TWAYNE'S WORLD AUTHORS SERIES

A Survey of the World's Literature

Sylvia Bowman, Indiana University
GENERAL EDITOR

GERMANY

Ulrich Weisstein, Indiana University
EDITOR

Alfred Döblin

(TWAS 290)

German Information Center

Alfred Döblin

Alfred Döblin

By WOLFGANG KORT
The Catholic University of America

Twayne Publishers, Inc. :: New York

Copyright © 1974 by Twayne Publishers, Inc.

All Rights Reserved

Library of Congress Cataloging in Publication Data
Kort, Wolfgang, 1939-
  Alfred Döblin.

  (Twayne world authors series, TWAS 290. Germany)
  Bibliography: p. 159.
  1. Döblin, Alfred, 1878-1957. I. Title.
PT2607.O35Z718   838'.9'1209   73-16222
ISBN 0-8057-2266-1

MANUFACTURED IN THE UNITED STATES OF AMERICA

For Ruth

Preface

Unfortunately, only two of Alfred Döblin's novels have been translated into English, namely his masterpiece *Berlin Alexanderplatz* and a little novel written in exile, *Pardon wird nicht gegeben* ("Pardon will not be granted," English title: *Men Without Mercy*). Of these two books only the first is still generally available.

While after the war American Germanists discovered Döblin almost before their German counterparts—as is demonstrated by a series of excellent dissertations to which this study is indebted—the interest of the general public is limited to *Berlin Alexanderplatz*.

This monograph—the first in English to attempt a study of Döblin's entire *oeuvre*—will seek to provide a general introduction to Döblin's life and work. Because of the limited space available and in the face of the scope of the works involved, this study can only attempt to establish some basic principles of interpretation. It is hoped, however, to awaken a general interest in an author who has a firm place in the literary history of the first half of this century, even though not all his works are widely familiar. Perhaps also, this study can compensate, in part, for the absence of English translations of the major works.

Döblin viewed himself as a writer of extended narratives and the greater part of his works consists of lengthy novels. Thus, his short stories and plays will only be mentioned in passing. The fact that more space is devoted to works written before emigration (1933) than to works written in exile and those of Döblin's old age is due to the difference in quality. This difference will be more fully explained in the course of the study.

The following abbreviations for Döblin's works will be used throughout: AB, *Alexanderplatz, Berlin. The Story of Franz Biberkopf*. Translated into the American by Eugene Jolas.—AD.

Im Buch..., *Alfred Döblin. Im Buch. Zu Haus. Auf der Strasse. Vorgestellt von Alfred Döblin und Oskar Loerke.*—Al, *Aufsätze zur Literatur.*—Am, *Amazonas.*—BMG, *Berge Meere und Giganten.*—Br, *Briefe.*—BW, *Babylonische Wandrung oder Hochmut kommt vor dem Fall.*—DnU, *Der neue Urwald* (Part III of the South America trilogy).—G, *Giganten. Ein Abenteuerbuch.*—Ha, *Hamlet oder die lange Nacht nimmt ein Ende.*—IüN, *Das Ich über der Natur.*—Ma, *Manas. Epische Dichtung.*—Nov. 18, I/II/III, *November 1918. Eine deutsche Revolution. Erzählwerk.* Volume I/II/III.—Pard, *Pardon wird nicht gegeben.*—RiP, *Reise in Polen.*—Sr, *Schicksalsreise. Bericht und Bekenntnis.*—SV, *Der schwarze Vorhang. Roman von den Worten und Zufällen.*—UD, *Unser Dasein.*—Wa, *Wallenstein.*—WaK, *Wadzeks Kampf mit der Dampfturbine.*—Wl, *Die drei Sprünge des Wang-Iun. Chinesischer Roman.*—Zl, *Die Zeitlupe.* Kleine Prosa aus dem Nachlass zusammengestellt von Walter Muschg.

WOLFGANG KORT

The Catholic University of America

Acknowledgments

I would like to thank the many friends and colleagues who made essential contributions to this book: Louis Huguet who let me read his detailed, but unfortunately still unpublished, *Habilitationsschrift* on Döblin; Anthony W. Riley and Joris Duytschaever who at present are both working on studies on Döblin and who contributed suggestions and valuable references to this monograph. I want especially to thank Dennis P. Krueger for his translation of the original German manuscript, and David M. Cussen and Mason Rossiter Smith for their proofreading and advice. With the exception of those taken from *Alexanderplatz, Berlin* all translations are our own. I thank the Viking Press, Inc., New York for permission to quote from *Alexanderplatz, Berlin* by Eugene Jolas, and the Walter Verlag Oten/Freiburg i. Br. for permission to quote from the works of Döblin now in print.

Contents

	Preface	7
	Acknowledgments	9
	Chronology	13
1.	The Life of a German Intellectual	17
2.	Literary Beginnings	34
3.	Theory of the Epic and Philosophy of Nature	43
4.	Imagination and Reality—China and Berlin	54
5.	History and Science Fiction	70
6.	Mythology and Modern Existence	90
7.	"Why Write, and for Whom?"—The Novels of Exile	110
8.	Return to Europe—The Novel *Hamlet*	136
9.	Conclusion	144
	Notes and References	147
	Selected Bibliography	159
	Index	163

Chronology

1878 Alfred Döblin born in Stettin (Pomerania), the second of five children.
1884 Entrance into the preparatory school of the municipal Friedrich-Wilhelm-Realgymnasium.
1888 Max Döblin, Alfred's father, deserts the family and travels with his mistress—twenty years his junior—to Hamburg and then to New York. Sophie Döblin, Alfred's mother, moves with the family to Berlin, where she is supported by one of her brothers. Alfred attends the elementary school.
1891 Attends the Köllnisches Gymnasium.
1900 Completes his *Gymnasium* schooling (*Abitur*). Begins studying medicine and philosophy in Berlin. "Jagende Rosse" (unpublished).
1902 Begins to write *Der schwarze Vorhang*.
1904 Continues studies in Freiburg im Breisgau. Further specialization in psychiatry and neurology.
1905 Under the pseudonym Alfred Börne, his play *Lydia und Mäxchen* is performed in Berlin. Completes medical degree with a dissertation entitled "Gedächtnisstörungen bei der Korsakoffschen Psychose" ("Disturbances of Memory in Korsakoff Psychosis"). Begins to work as an intern at the district insane asylum Prüll near Regensburg (Kreisirrenanstalt Prüll). Writes "Gespräche mit Kalypso über die Musik."
1906 Returns to Berlin to work at the psychiatric hospital Berlin-Buch.
1910 Co-founder of *Der Sturm* (Expressionistic journal). Acquaintance with Erna Reiss, his future wife. Trip to Belgium.
1911 Opens a practice in the Eastern part of Berlin.

1912 Marries Erna Reiss. Futurist Exposition in Berlin. Begins to write *Die drei Sprünge des Wang-lun*. Son Peter born.
1913 Publication of the first volume of novellas, *Die Ermordung einer Butterblume*. Begins *Wadzeks Kampf mit der Dampfturbine*.
1914 Military doctor in Saargemünd (Lorraine), after 1917 in Hagenau (Alsace).
1915 Son Wolfgang born.
1916 Begins work on *Wallenstein*.
1917 Publication of the second volume of novellas, *Die Lobensteiner reisen nach Böhmen*. Son Klaus born.
1918 Returns to Berlin. Joins the Independent Social Democrats (USPD).
1920 Publication of *Wallenstein*.
1921 Switches to the Socialist Party of Germany (SPD). Acquaintance with Yolla Niclas. Publishes *Der deutsche Maskenball* under the pen name Linke Poot.
1922 Receives the Kleist Prize.
1923 Performance of his play *Die Nonnen von Kemnade* in Leipzig.
1924 Trip to Poland. Publication of *Berge Meere und Giganten*. Is elected first president of the Protection League of German Writers (Schutzverband deutscher Schriftsteller). Becomes a member of the Society of Friends of New Russia (Gesellschaft der Freunde des neuen Russlands).
1925 *Reise in Polen* published. Founding of *Gruppe 1925*.
1926 Son Stefan born. Trip to France.
1927 Publication of *Manas. Epische Dichtung* and *Das Ich über der Natur*.
1928 On the occasion of his fiftieth birthday, *Alfred Döblin. Im Buch. Zu Haus. Auf der Strasse* appears, presented by Döblin and Oskar Loerke. Döblin is elected to the Dichter-Akademie der Preussischen Akademie der Künste. Leaves the SPD. Begins work on *Berlin Alexanderplatz*.
1929 *Berlin Alexanderplatz* published.
1930 Broadcast of a radio play based on *Berlin Alexanderplatz*.
1931 Film version of the novel with Heinrich George in the role of Biberkopf. Publication of *Wissen und Verändern! Offene Briefe an einen jungen Menschen*.
1932 *Giganten. Ein Abenteuerbuch*.

Chronology

1933 Publication of *Unser Dasein* and *Jüdische Erneuerung*. Escape to Switzerland, later to France.
1935 *Pardon wird nicht gegeben* and *Flucht und Sammlung des Judenvolkes* published. Founding of the Ligue Juive pour Colonisation.
1937 Publication of *Das Land ohne Tod*, Part I: *Die Fahrt ins Land ohne Tod*. Beginning of work on *November 1918*.
1938 *Das Land ohne Tod*, Part II: *Der blaue Tiger*.
1939 Works (as a naturalized French citizen) with Jean Giraudoux in France's information ministry. *Eine deutsche Revolution*, Part I: *Bürger und Soldaten 1918* published.
1940 Escape via France, Spain, and Portugal to New York and then to Hollywood. As a French soldier, Wolfgang Döblin dies in battle. The *Living Thoughts of Confucius* published with an introduction by Alfred Döblin. Begins to write *Schicksalsreise*.
1941 Conversion to Roman Catholicism.
1945 Returns to Paris, then to Baden-Baden, where he works in the cultural department of the French Military Government.
1946 Publication of *Der unsterbliche Mensch* and *Der Oberst und der Dichter*. Founding of the magazine *Das goldene Tor*. Starts work on *Hamlet*.
1948 Publishes *Der neue Urwald* (Part III of the South America trilogy) and *Unsere Sorge der Mensch*. Publication of the trilogy *November 1918* (1948–1950).
1949 Moves to Mainz. Co-founder and vice-president of the Mainz Akademie der Wissenschaften und der Literatur.
1951 Returns to Paris.
1956 *Hamlet oder die lange Nacht nimmt ein Ende*.
1957 Döblin dies in the psychiatric clinic in Emmendingen in the Black Forest and is buried in the cemetery of Housseras beside his son Wolfgang.

CHAPTER 1

The Life of a German Intellectual

DÖBLIN was always an enemy of personal revelation, for in the personal he sensed a lyrical subjectivity which he despised. Consequently, he was not a man to choose to write about himself, except in one specific form: that of a detached retrospect, preserving the objectivity of the epic poet, or the scientist even, toward the events of his own life. In 1922 he wrote: "I can't say anything about my spiritual development. Because I am myself engaged in psychoanalysis I know how wrong every self-revelation is. I am, besides, psychologically a touch-me-not. . . ."[1] Döblin admitted that he occasionally saw himself forced to issue autobiographical statements, but his attempt at an autobiography—begun in 1918 when he was in the middle of his life—petered out after several pages. Characteristically, Döblin switched very quickly from first- to third-person narration.[2] To a series of autobiographical sketches, published on the occasion of his fiftieth birthday, he added a graphological anaylsis, instead of a thorough self-analysis.[3] He also thought it necessary to apologize for his book *Schicksalsreise* by saying that it had become "merely a personal book."[4] Direct autobiographical references in his works are rare. The letters which have been published up to now are reserved to the point of rebuffing the reader. Only with the softening of old age and the increasing strain of isolation in exile do they occasionally open a view into the inner, personal, and private man. Döblin seldom helps the biographer of his internal history. One is, therefore, limited to the factual aspects.

Döblin was born in Stettin on August 10, 1878. At the age of ten, he moved to Berlin. In a retrospect written in 1928, he called this move his real birth. Obviously, he preferred to consider the first decade he spent at Stettin unimportant.[5] The earlier family tragedy, which had furnished the reason for moving to Berlin, was a traumatic experience for Döblin. His concern with it occu-

[17]

pies by far the greatest space in "Erster Rückblick," and vestiges of it are still clearly visible in *Pardon wird nicht gegeben*, "a family novel with autobiographical elements," and even in his last novel *Hamlet oder die lange Nacht nimmt ein Ende*. What had happened?

After many years of marital strife, Döblin's forty-two-year-old father had deserted his family for a girl twenty years younger than himself and had fled, first to Hamburg and then to America. The family, consisting of four sons—Alfred being the second youngest—and a daughter, was penniless and had to spend many years paying off the father's debts.

Three times in his "Autobiographische Skizze" Döblin considered this decisive turning point in his youth. Each time he chose a different point of view. First he described the dissolution of his family in the ironic-objective tone of Franz Biberkopf, the hero of *Berlin Alexanderplatz*. In the second instance, he spoke as the son of his mother: strong accusations were levelled against the father who had so irresponsibly rid himself of the duties to his large family. Most revealing, however, is the third instance. Entangled in an imaginary psychoanalytical dialogue with himself, Döblin is pained to relive the events once more, and this time in their broadest scope. He presses beyond immediate and easy moral judgments to the true sources of the tragedy, i.e., to its social and ethnic factors. Both parents were of Jewish descent, but what an unbridgeable distance there was between his father and his mother! She came from an industrious, pragmatic, sober merchant family, proud of its success and money. The mother brought these qualities to the marriage. The father, who was forced into the marriage by his parents—Sophie Freudenheim was a good catch—was the exact opposite: a gentle, instinctive man, but very gifted. He was a composer and gave his children their first music lessons, wrote occasional verse, and sketched. But he had no ambition and no success. His ready-made clothes shop failed, and he opened a tailor's shop instead:

My mother didn't have much respect for him. She called him her 'educated lackey.' A mean expression. It was a bad story, this merchant and money pride in my mother's family. They were all vivacious, active, practical people, good earners and even an occasional *bon vivant*.

The Life of a German Intellectual

Anything beyond that was unknown. Or rather, not merely unknown, but ridiculous. A cause for mockery and irony.[6]

Döblin, who knew full well where his artistic talent originated, shows here a greater understanding of his father's situation. Due to the antithesis of bourgeois sobriety and artistic inclination, the marriage was bound to break up. This antithesis had long-lasting effects on Döblin. On the one hand, he took his career as a doctor seriously; on the other hand, he initially had the bad conscience of a bourgeois merchant about his writing; it was something forbidden:

> I can speak about it because I have personally become acquainted with this scorn, this narrow-mindedness, this bitter, arrogant severity. I would not have dared, not dreamed of daring, to show my writings at home. For many years, nobody at home knew that I was writing. And when, in 1906, a little play of mine—along with one by Paul Scheerbart—was performed in a matinee, it did not appear under my name, the name of my family, but under a pseudonym.[7]

Previously, Döblin had lost the manuscript of his novel "Die jagenden Rosse," sent under a pseudonym to the critic Fritz Mauthner, because he had not dared to reveal his real identity. "I had a bad conscience about my works. The experience had impressed itself so strongly. Unto the second generation."[8]

For the now impoverished family, the move to Berlin meant a step down the social ladder. The Döblins often changed their residence but always lived east of Alexanderplatz, in the Eastern part of Berlin, a worker's district full of smoke and factories.

> The most terrible thing I saw is called the housing shortage—at least that is its name. There is nothing quite like bureaucratic clichés. They exceed those of the poets. Until my fourteenth year I slept with my brother in one bed in a windowless room in the Eastern section of the city. (Later my brother and his wife were gassed by the promulgators of a new progress.) [9]

The family survived with the help of Mrs. Döblin's brothers, who had a thriving lumber business, and because of the industry of the oldest son, Ludwig, who became the head of the household.

When the family catastrophe occurred, Döblin had just entered the Sexta (the first grade in high school). He was taken out of

[19]

school and taught by a private tutor. In Berlin he first attended the district school at Friedrichshain (Gemeindeschule am Friedrichshain); three years later he entered the Köllnisches Gymnasium as a scholarship holder. Döblin always remembered his school days with aversion, even hatred. The fact that he was always three years older than his classmates surely did not improve his situation. Nor was his interest in Kleist and Hölderlin or his readings of Schopenhauer and Spinoza (outsiders not belonging to the accepted curriculum) well received. Yet on occasion he was prepared to admit that he owed much to his *Gymnasium* training: Prussian sobriety and discipline, and a solidly based classical education. Nonetheless, Leo Kreutzer is surely correct when he traces Döblin's alienation, his skepticism toward state, party, and church as institutions, his frequently anarchic traits, and his inclination toward extreme, contradictory intellectual positions to the family tragedy and to his school days.[10]

After his *Abitur* (final high school examination) in 1900, Döblin began to study medicine and philosophy in Berlin. When he later wrote that none of the literature of this period appealed to him, but that natural science and medicine captivated him to an extraordinary degree, this was only half true, because in this instance, the view of the doctor dominated that of the author. He actually took an active interest in literary events:

In 1900, at the end of my school years and the beginning of my university studies, I came into contact with Herwarth Walden (he, too, lived in the Eastern section of Berlin in the Holzmarktstrasse; his father was a doctor). We made fun of the current idols of the bourgeoisie, of Gerhart Hauptmann with his counterfeit, fairy-tale spooks, of the classicist constipation of Stefan George. There was also the author of *Buddenbrooks* at that time. He was not in the picture. We met Else Lasker-Schüler and Peter Hille in the Café des Westens, occasionally at Dalbelli's by the Potsdam bridge. We rubbed shoulders with Richard Dehmel, Wedekind, and Scheerbart.[11]

As the first chairman of the literary section of the "Finken," a fraternity, he organized soirées with authors. Thus, there can really be no question of a dislike for literary activities. But Döblin's remark brings into relief—as do many others—the problem of his double life as a doctor and poet.

The Life of a German Intellectual

In 1904, Döblin went to Freiburg im Breisgau to complete his studies. This placid provincial town near the Black Forest was quite different from the German capital bristling with activity, and consequently, Döblin seems to have been quite lonely and isolated. In Freiburg he engaged in a fleeting love affair resulting in a child that died shortly after birth. Although this event appears to have left no lasting mark on him, it could have been the autobiographical skeleton of Döblin's important story "Die Ermordung einer Butterblume" ("The Murder of a Buttercup").[12]

Döblin finished his medical studies with a psychiatric thesis "Gedächtnisstörungen bei der Korsakoffschen Psychose" ("Disturbances of Memory in Korsakoff Psychosis"). After taking his degree in 1905, he went to the district insane asylum near Regensburg (Kreisirrenanstalt), where he was chiefly involved in psychiatry.

In 1906, he returned to Berlin where he worked as an intern, first at the psychiatric hospital Berlin-Buch. He continued to study psychiatry, spent his nights conducting biological experiments, and published a series of scientific articles. On top of all these professional duties and interests, he kept on producing shorter literary works. These years—apart from being important for his career as a physician and writer—also played a major role in his personal life. In Berlin-Buch, Döblin had a love affair with a very young Protestant nurse who gave birth to a child. But he did not want, or dare, to marry her—perhaps because of his mother's veto. When, later on, he was working as an intern in a municipal hospital (Städtisches Krankenhaus Urban) in Berlin, he met his future wife, Erna Reiss, also a medical student. She was the daughter of a well-to-do Jewish merchant—like Döblin's mother, Sophie Freudenheim, a good catch![13] Before Döblin became officially engaged to Erna Reiss in 1911, he confessed the affair with the nurse to her. He was stunned to learn from her that she, too, had expected a child but had had an abortion in Belgium. This coincidence becomes even stranger when it is noted that Döblin had visited the World's Fair in Brussels at the same time! His marriage was a very difficult one, yet Döblin was incapable of breaking the tie—the overly strong maternal bond on a new level. Thus, the traumatic experience of his parent's marriage was to be repeated in his own. The shocks of the years 1910 and 1911 form the disguised autobiographical nucleus of a number of stories written at that time. The tensions of his marriage are still evident in Döblin's last novel, *Hamlet oder die lange Nacht nimmt ein Ende* ("Hamlet or the Long Night Comes to an End").

In 1911, Döblin had opened his own private practice in the Eastern part of the city—not an easy task under any circumstances! The following year he married Erna Reiss, and their first son, Peter, was born. And yet, during this period, in spite of all the difficulties of his situation, Döblin managed to write his first lengthy epic work: *Die drei Sprünge des Wang-lun* ("The Three Leaps of Wang-lun"). For him this novel marked the breakthrough of literary productivity:

It was almost a dam break. *Wang-lun,* almost two volumes in the original, was written—including the preliminary work—in eight months; poured out on the elevated train, at the emergency station, during night service, between two consultations, on the stairs during a house call; it was finished in May, 1913.[14]

Even the First World War, during which Döblin worked as a military doctor in Saargemünd (Lorraine) and in Hagenau (Alsace), could not stop this literary productivity. On the contrary, in his leisure time he wrote another of his masterpieces: the voluminous novel *Wallenstein*. Although *Wang-lun* already had a decided political-social side, it was through *Wallenstein* that Döblin became increasingly aware of the political implications of this war and in articles and glosses began to express himself fairly regularly about political events.

In his first letters about the war, a nationalistic tone, surprising in Döblin, is conspicuous. The article "Reims," in which he takes a position on the controversy over the bombardment of the Cathedral of Reims, is a tirade of hate against England.[15] But there is no lack of humanitarian insight into the absurdity of war: the controversy over the destroyed windows of the church, although carried on in the name of culture, is barbaric in the face of the thousands who fell in battle.

Döblin's rather uncritical attitude toward the German situation soon gave way to a greater pensiveness. "It seems that I'm coming to my senses," he wrote in 1917.[16] Of very decisive importance in this respect were the reports of the Russian revolution. Döblin saw the events in Russia as a new proof of the everlasting strug-

The Life of a German Intellectual

gle of mankind for humanity and justice—and gratefully remembered the influence Tolstoy and Dostoevski had exerted on him:

> When this Revolution happened, reminiscences from peaceful times stirred in me. These "Russian" ideas, so joyful, young, and hearty, appeared everywhere, and, again and again, where the living human spirit broke a path through strong material, soulless, and insufferable resistance. In the old days, they accompanied the Bundschuh [peasant's shoe, banner of peasant revolts] and the German peasants, even though Luther railed against them and called them wild beasts that should be clubbed to death. They fought for the fundamentals of Christianity and upheld them against the letter-of-the-law attitude, against delusions of law and presumption, and against self-satisfied hypocrisy. They were audible in the noise at the Paulskurche in Frankfurt [German National Convention in 1848]. They will never reach fulfillment, will always sound the alarm. Again and again, mankind degenerates, again and again the warning sign appears on the wall. When mankind wants to rejuvenate itself, it bathes in this fountain.[17]

Döblin at once realized the meaning of this event: "Nothing that this generation has experienced can be, I believe, compared with this moment for greatness."[18]

In Germany, Döblin saw only the apathy of the "men of the mind" ("die Geistigen"). But he also thought that he saw a new people's community formed by the war, and that the memory of Napoleon's wars of liberation and of Kleist's *Hermannschlacht* had surfaced. Thus, he tried to shake the "men of the mind" into activity, into battle for the proletariat whose leaders they should be:

> The war is seeking to become spiritual. The others whom it concerns have known about it for a long time, but you, disinherited and suicidals, proletarians beyond all proletarians, know nothing. Thoughts challenge your souls and heads. They call you, so that you can be midwives at their birth. The world is in ferment, the dough is rising; where are the bakers? How many-sided and vacillating these ideas are, how dangerously weak, and how close to pale romanticism and ridiculousness. How strong, massive, healthy the opposite ideas, how close to plain barbarity, to naked, fresh power. And now might against might, many mights against many mights. Fighters are needed. Where are you? [19]

How bitter the disappointment must have been for a man who had started with such hopes!

Even at the end of the war, Döblin was still a nationalist, who vehemently and eloquently justified Germany's position. If he looked longingly toward Russia, he looked skeptically at the three Western democracies, France, England, and America. If the specter of feudalism was still visible in Germany, he also saw outmoded and unsuccessful politics in the democratic countries, as manifested in the conditions of peace. In Döblin's eyes, their position contradicted their democratic form of government and, beyond that, provided the incipient German democracy with a bad example.[20]

Döblin, who was still in Alsace when the revolution of November, 1918, broke out,[21] greeted the young republic on the basis of its democracy and its civic spirit joyfully and enthusiastically; he knew where he belonged. When Richard Dehmel asked him to sign a proclamation which contained pejorative remarks about the revolution he wrote:

You will understand that I am totally unable to speak disparagingly of the "brawl" of our "men of revolution" or of the "robber guild" of the League of Nations, etc.; that's barking up the wrong tree, in my opinion: I am, and remain, absolutely blind and deaf. But I do not doubt where I have to place myself in the final leg of the race between socialism and imperialism—and that is the core of our difference, which I heartily regret.[22]

He makes his position even more unmistakably clear when he remarks to Efraim Frisch, the editor of the *Neue Merkur*, that blood red, symbolizing revolution and socialism, is his color.[23] Döblin joined the Independent Social Democratic Party (USPD) in 1918 and was a member of the Social Democratic Party (SPD) for several years after the USPD split at its convention in Halle (1921). But his initial enthusiasm soon gave way to sobriety and skepticism. He soon recognized the growing political indifference of the masses, and especially their move to the right. He saw old powers being resurrected, "the dusk through which something shines like a uniform and a helmet."[24] He emphasized that the revolution had not yet created a perfect republic, but only the possibility of one. He demanded criticism and "liberation from the terror of idols."[25] And there was also no lack of unhappiness

The Life of a German Intellectual

on his part with the inactivity of the "men of the mind": "The German citizens who call themselves intellectuals do not count. They consider lyricism as a political factor. Their uselessness and harmlessness is the only thing that can be counted on for sure."[26]

At the same time, Döblin's biting satirical glosses on the age appeared in the *Neue Rundschau* under the pseudonym "Linke Poot" (Left Paw); later they were collected in the book *Der deutsche Maskenball* ("The German Masquerade"). Here, Döblin airs his irritation at the abuses practiced in the young republic and its organs, at the clergy, and at the resurrected reactionary powers. Later Franz Biberkopf provides Döblin's final judgment on the Weimar Republic in the striking formulation: "You always make revolution with your mugs; your republic is nothing but an industrial accident." (AB, 102). That it is Döblin who speaks in this passage can be shown by his merciless description of the events in *November 1918*, which will be discussed later. In Döblin's view, the political parties with their murky slogans have taken the place of the old Junker regime: "We have in the present parliamentarianism just as insufferable a leadership as the former one which supported itself by conquest, inheritance, and the divine right of kings, whereas the latter works by sanctioned deception according to a plan."[27] By contrast, Döblin propagates the idea of the Soviets as a means of self-help for the masses against foreign and autocratic governments. More freedom, he felt, was only possible by decentralizing the state's structure. He was surely influenced by Kropotkin and Bakunin in this idea. But the Soviets, too, are likely to succumb to the process of ideologization by the parties. Yet Döblin believes that the thought of an "ethic socialism" is, in the long run, irresistible: "The free form of a state which, at this time, can only be the republic is the prerequisite for the development of a communal structure."[28] Despite all reservations, Döblin affirmed the idea of the republic and of socialism and called for an alliance with the workers: "Friends of the republic and of freedom. Move to the left. To the side of the workers."[29]

His disappointment at the failure of the revolution and the alliance of the young republic with the reactionary forces of yesterday did not drive Döblin to complete retreat into inwardness. To be sure, after 1921 hardly any political essays issued from his pen. As a physician in Eastern Berlin with three children—a

[25]

fourth was born in 1926—his economic situation was precarious. From 1921 to 1924 he wrote theater reviews for the *Prager Tageblatt* to assure himself of a steady source of income.[30] In 1921 he also made the acquaintance of Charlotte (Yolla) Niclas, who became his muse from then on. Another event which drew him away from politics was his journey to Poland, undertaken in 1924 and recorded in a book by that title.[31] Christianity and Judaism—these are the two experiences which moved and shook him on this trip. As much as he criticized the atavism in the life and attitude of the Jews in Warsaw's ghetto, and as much as their condition insulted his progressive sense, the Jews, by this very fact, became a symbol for the persisting power of the ego. On the other hand, the crucified Christ symbolized never-ending human misery and suffering. Thus, a need for spiritual orientation and religion was stirred up again by this trip which was to have a long-lasting effect on his life and work. For henceforth he concerns himself less with masses and mass movements (as he did especially in *Berge Meere und Giganten:* "Mountains Seas and Giants," 1924) and more with the individual and his problems.

With Döblin's growing reputation in the mid- and late 1920's came official recognition. When in 1926 the Dresden Staatsoper performed Verdi's *Forza del Destino* in a new translation by Franz Werfel, the official representatives of the younger German writers at this noteworthy event were Bertolt Brecht, Arnolt Bronnen, and Alfred Döblin.[32] In the same year, Döblin acted as a judge of narrative literature for a literary contest sponsored by the magazine *Die literarische Welt*.[33] In 1928 he was elected to the Prussian Academy of the Arts, Section for Literature.[34] As always, he attempted to provoke discussions by his unorthodox thinking. He also tried to build bridges between writers and literary critics and for that reason established a liaison with the Germanist Julius Petersen in Berlin which was not too productive, however.

Although at the time Döblin was not without a following, he was hardly a popular writer; his two most recent works, *Manas* and *Das Ich über der Natur* ("The Ego above Nature"), did not sell at all. "I am understood poorly and with difficulty these days . . . ," he complained to Ferdinand Lion.[35] But when he wrote these disconsolate words, he was working on the novel

The Life of a German Intellectual

which would assure his fame not only in Germany, but in the entire world: *Berlin Alexanderplatz*. Döblin's masterpiece was published in 1929, the year of the world depression which constituted a decisive factor in Hitler's rise to power. Less than four years later, its author, being a Jew and a left-wing intellectual, had to leave Germany.

Döblin was a member of the Schutzverband deutscher Schriftsteller (Protective Alliance of German Writers) and was nominated to its executive committee in 1920. In 1925, some left-wing and Communist writers formed the Group 25 (Gruppe 25). The radical Communist writers, among them Johannes R. Becher, split off from this group and formed the Bund proletarisch-revolutionärer Schriftsteller Deutschlands (Union of Proletarian Revolutionary Writers of Germany) in 1927. The organ of this union, the *Linkskurve*, made a sharp attack on *Berlin Alexanderplatz* and prevented its appearance in Russia.

In the view of the *Linkskurve*, Döblin's book was counterrevolutionary because it was opposed to the class struggle; in addition, the hero was not a worker. On the contrary, the worker was scorned, or at least this is how the *Linkskurve* saw it. Döblin answered with his article "Katastrophe in einer Linkskurve".[36] He criticized the spokesmen of the Bund, especially Johannes R. Becher, for their unrealistic position which surfaced in the unaltered Expressionist language that Döblin felt he had long since left behind.[37] From this controversy between the formerly allied left-wing bourgeois and the Communist writers, there arose, following an open letter by Gustav René Hocke the future Romanist, a Döblin circle in which the political, social, and intellectual problems of the day were discussed. As a consequence, in 1931, Döblin published his most important political essay: *Wissen und Verändern! Offene Briefe an einen jungen Menschen* ("Know and Change! Open Letters to a Young Man"). It begins in the form of letters written to Hocke, who had addressed himself to Döblin with a request for help in intellectual and political orientation; but it then, characteristically, turns more and more into a soliloquy.

The basic ideas of the book *Wissen und Verändern!* are familiar from the articles mentioned earlier and show how constant Döblin's views remained. The "Geistigen" ("men of the mind")—the concept "intellectual" was apparently too narrow for

[27]

him—are challenged to take the side of the workers, who must decisively free themselves from the anachronistic ideology of class struggle. How relevant Döblin's theses have remained! From the point of view of his philosophy of nature, which denies any materialism and emphasizes intellectual principles, Döblin criticizes the position of Marxism. In Döblin's opinion, Marxism, from a solid scientific basis, attacked and unmasked capitalism but relied too much on economic factors and the class struggle. An essential aid in the argument with Marxism came from the lectures by the unorthodox Marxist Karl Korsch which he—along with Brecht—attended. Like Döblin himself, Korsch, liked the idea of the Soviets.

What makes these letters so characteristic of Döblin is his wavering attitude toward action, connecting this book with his literary works in which the dialectics of revolution and submission are a constant theme. Döblin wants a whole, free, natural man— that is the sense of his "ethic socialism." He wants an organic, not a forced collective. He also knows that these goals can only be realized in battle against feudalism and private capitalism. But he demands knowledge, which he finds lacking in most of those whom he addresses. From this knowledge, the changing activity would arise by itself. But the difficulty of this position was apparent as soon as Döblin was urged by his group to make a public statement. He declined, for in his often expressed mistrust of the parties occupying the old positions of power he could not enter the camp of any party, especially not in the political confusion of the 1930's. His program of "ethic socialism" was nonpartisan. At the same time, he was only too aware of the absence of any resonance between the intellectuals and the people. At the moment when every call was for action and decision, he wanted to go on talking. The knowledge was there, but—like so many of the figures in his novels—Döblin preferred not to accept the challenge to change things. His wish to affirm and preserve the generally human, the humane, in the form of a deep and stable ego-nature relationship collided with the political-social questions of the day which demanded a clear commitment to a party platform. Mistrustful of partisan politics (*"Bonzenwirtschaft"*) from way back, Döblin could not, and did not, want to make such a commitment.

Like many others, Döblin underestimated the gravity of the

The Life of a German Intellectual

situation. On February 15, 1933, the chairman of the literary section of the Prussian Academy of the Arts, Heinrich Mann, who, together with Käthe Kollwitz, had signed a public statement calling for the formation of a people's front of the SPD and KPD (Communist Party of Germany), was forced to resign from the Academy.[38] Once again Döblin, as a free and independent intellectual, raised his voice and criticized the reasons for this exclusion. On February 28, immediately after the Reichstag fire, upon the warning and urging of his friends, among them the French Ambassador, François-Poncet, and his publisher, Fischer, he left Germany. He believed that his stay in Switzerland, where he was the guest of the famous psychiatrist, Ludwig Binswanger, would only be of short duration. He did not suspect that twelve years would pass before his return home. He wrote to his friend and colleague Oskar Loerke that he had "left Berlin for a short while because of the bad weather in Northern Germany."[39] But that was an error; all too soon Döblin had to admit that for him, as an intellectual of the left and as a Jew, to return to Germany under this regime would be impossible. On May 10, his books were among those that were publicly burned. His wife and his youngest son, Stefan, soon followed him into exile. Toward the end of the year, Döblin left expensive Switzerland, where he probably did not feel comfortable, and settled near Paris. The temporary sojourn had become a permanent condition.

Döblin's flight from Germany marks a sharp break not only in his external life. In the beginning of his exile, he was able to continue living on a modest scale with his family. Later on, after he had to flee from France to the USA, his economic situation became more and more precarious, since in neither country was he allowed to practice medicine. Other problems added their weight, including the language barrier. In his theoretical writings, Döblin always stressed the importance of a living language for the writer, and *Berlin Alexanderplatz* is the best illustration of this thesis. But he was in a German-speaking country only for a short time; subsequently he was excluded from a normal contact with his native language. He had learned French in school, even though his school lessons had concentrated on the passive mastery of that language, and in Paris he made a great effort to revive and improve his French. But he was never properly at home in that language. Later, in California, his situation was not much better. The loss of a public and the difficulty of finding a publisher were no less depressing. Why should he continue to write? And for whom?

Above all, for Döblin as for so many other writers, the exile was a time of deep inner crisis which culminated in his complete breakdown in 1940, when he had to flee from advancing German troops, and which paved the way for his conversion. All his convictions, his belief in humanity and the triumph of reason, his hope for a just social and political order, and even his philosophy of nature had been shattered by the rise of Fascism and the outbreak of World War II.

But, unlike many of his colleagues who, in utter despair, committed suicide, Döblin accepted the challenge of this completely changed situation. He continued to write and took active part in the intellectual resistance to Fascism and in organizing the Jews, although his contacts with the Jewish tradition were none too strong. He was a co-founder of the Ligue Juive pour Colonisation which revived old territorial plans. He worked on the magazine *Friedland*, gave lectures, and even learned Yiddish. With the brochures *Jüdische Erneuerung* ("Jewish Renewal") and *Flucht und Sammlung des Judenvolkes* ("Flight and Collection of the Jewish People") he entered public discussion of the Jewish question.

However, on the one hand his picture of Jewry was limited to the Eastern Jews that he had become acquainted with on his journey to Poland; on the other hand, as always, he was concerned not so much with narrow political goals as with the whole man, a concept that had hindered his energetic intervention just after *Wissen und Verändern!* for fear of one-sided partisanship. Very early Döblin wrote to Isidor Lipschitz: "I'm only half glad about the League because it stresses 'country' too one-sidedly and does not attack, in my opinion, the central theme of man and of general Jewish renewal."[40] He wanted—and here again we have one of Döblin's general themes—to force the Jews closer to "nature." But Döblin despaired of the individualism of the Jews and felt that a great common movement was lacking. Thus, about 1938, one hope poorer, he gave up his collaboration on these undertakings which had consumed a good deal of his time.

As early as 1936, he had become a French citizen, not least of all because he had two draft-age sons, Klaus-Claude and Wolf-

The Life of a German Intellectual

gang-Vincent. His oldest son, Peter, was in London preparing to move to New York, while the youngest, Stefan, was still with his parents and in school. In 1939, Döblin worked with a group of Germanists at the French Ministry of Information under Jean Giraudoux. One of his closest friendships was with the French Germanist, Robert Minder.

But although Döblin seems to have got back on his feet, Paris was only a stage in his exile, for the German invasion forced him to flee to the USA. In his autobiographical book *Schicksalsreise* ("Journey of Fate"), he describes the terrible flight through France, his separation from wife and child, their unexpected reunion, and his physical and psychic collapse at Mende.

With the help of friends and their oldest son, Peter, already working in New York, the Döblins went via Lisbon and New York to Hollywood, California, where a large number of German refugees were living. Among them were such celebrities as the Mann brothers, Bertolt Brecht, Franz Werfel, Lion Feuchtwanger, and others. Here, Döblin formally converted to the Roman Catholic faith. An important factor in his decision was the school attendance of his youngest son, Stefan. While, on the whole, positively oriented toward American pragmatism and community spirit, Döblin felt that these values did not accomplish enough for the spiritual and intellectual side of man. He enrolled his youngest son in a Jesuit school and decided, after long discussions with the priests, to convert—a step which must have alienated many of his friends and increased his solitude.

The position of the aging writer in Hollywood was hardly enviable. Like many German emigrants, he wrote scripts for Metro-Goldwyn-Mayer. Although he had been interested in movies prior to this time and had already written a film script,[41] he did not adjust well and considered his work at the studios as a pure waste of time, especially because none of his suggestions were accepted or used and because for him the whole business was aimed too much at pure consumerism. After a year, his contract was terminated and, from then on, his family had to rely on donations of committees and aid societies—always an uncertain business. Added to the financial difficulties were health problems and, above all his worry about Wolfgang Döblin. This extraordinarily gifted mathematician had been killed in 1940 as a French soldier, but his parents did not learn of his death until

1945. Above all, Döblin suffered—as he had in France—from the language barrier.[42] Even within the group of German-speaking emigrants he seems to have isolated himself. He had a tense relationship with several of them, especially Thomas Mann.[43] His conversion and especially his convert's attitude must have offended many of the emigrants. Since his arrival in America, practically no works of his had been printed. "I am writing like an eighteen-year-old, only for myself."[44] That the Marxists and Stalinists among the emigrants had taken over the political leadership must have embittered this man who had always sought to overcome class ideology and had always affirmed the idea of a just and humane social order over ephemeral party programs. Under these circumstances, Döblin must have felt tempted to retreat into inwardness.

After the war, Döblin almost immediately returned to France and thence to Germany, to work in the cultural department of the French Military Government in Baden-Baden. He wrote unceasingly, as was his habit. Besides his activities as a reader and censor, he had to lay the foundation of a magazaine which appeared from 1946 to 1951 under the title *Das goldene Tor* ("The Golden Gate").[45] Döblin set his sights on making this magazine a place for the exiled and unjustly forgotten: "To let exiled literature return, to present and contribute to the new literature that came as far as it came, as much as a magazine can, to reproduce a healthy and normal condition in the literary life of our country" (Sr, 404). But Döblin could not find a common meeting ground with the three great figures of German literature who formed a bridge spanning the Nazi period: he had always found Thomas Mann unacceptable; in Gottfried Benn he saw only the cynic and the nihilist; and with Brecht it was impossible to regain the earlier friendly relationship. The deeper reason for this failure of understanding was probably that Döblin overexposed the Christian and anti-Marxist side of his attitude and easily insulted others with his overly critical attitude. The same is true of his relationship with Johannes R. Becher. Here, too, his attempt to invoke a common, humane cause fell on deaf ears—a situation similar to that of the 1930's. With an energy admirable for his age, Döblin tried to stimulate the slowly burgeoning cultural life. He helped to refound the Mainzer Akademie, travelled about the country, professed his Christianity pub-

The Life of a German Intellectual

licly, and gave lectures. That the former intellectual of the left, who had vehemently attacked the Church and the clergy in the 1920's, now stood and spoke before them as a Christian must have seemed incredible to many. The reaction was mixed, but mostly negative. About his visit to Berlin Döblin wrote:

> I talked in Berlin about how organization devours and spoils the spirit and gave all sorts of examples and did not omit the ultimate example: how socialism deteriorated into a governmental structure and decayed to political favoritism. And what was to be done now. For me there was no question about the answer. People would have to press beyond formulations such as "socialism" to the basic values. People have to go to the real source, back to this real source. I called humility the necessary basic attitude after the arrogant pride which had preceded it. I spoke openly about it, and also about praying. (Sr, 456)

These words clearly show how little Döblin's political and philosophical attitudes had changed in comparison with the time before his emigration. After quoting a series of negative and skeptical voices, Döblin continues: "Later, at a reception, I saw a number of writers who lived in Berlin; some of them I knew. There was no real contact. Besides, I answered one greeting in a way that many did not like" (Sr, 457). His occasional appearance in the uniform of a French colonel also must have caused some alienation.

Again Döblin felt misunderstood and silenced because he found no publisher for many of his writings. With growing concern he watched the political scene, the cold war and, still worse, the assertion of reactionary, or even neo-Fascist, faces in Germany. Depressed by what he experienced, and with the bitter feeling of not being heard, of not counting, he emigrated for a second time to Paris in 1953. His rapidly deteriorating health, a progressive lameness that required intensive care, occasioned his return to sanitariums in the Black Forest. He lived to see the fiftieth anniversary of his doctoral exam in the Freiburg clinic. In 1957 he died in a sanitarium in Emmendingen in the Black Forest. He is buried in Housseras in the Vosges mountains beside his son Wolfgang.

CHAPTER 2

Literary Beginnings

DÖBLIN has often stated that he wrote when he was in school, "already poetizing as a schoolboy."[1] As yet there exists no exact chronology of the works written during his school and university days, or even of the later works. Not all of them have been published, and many are undated. At fourteen, at any rate, Döblin was writing sketches, essays, stories, and later on, two short novels.

During his years at the university in Berlin, besides his professional concern with medicine and natural sciences, Döblin engaged in particularly intensive studies of Hegel under Georg Lasson. The favorite authors of his school days, Kleist and Hölderlin, were supplemented by two new discoveries of long-lasting effect: Nietzsche (*Genealogy of Morals*) and Dostoevski (*Crime and Punishment*), whom Döblin viewed as a predecessor of Freud. In 1902 and 1903 he wrote two unpublished essays about Nietzsche: "Der Wille zur Macht als Erkenntnis bei Friedrich Nietzsche" ("The Will to Power as Insight in Friedrich Nietzsche") and "Zu Nietzsches Morallehre" ("Concerning Views on Morality"). As a Hegelian philosopher, he criticized Nietzsche's agnosticism. A strong need for knowledge and a metaphysical system is clearly evident. His simultaneous interest in music, especially in Richard Wagner (whose influence can be seen on every page of the *Erzählungen*), Johannes Brahms, and Hugo Wolf, flowed later into his esthetics of music ("Gespräche mit Kalypso über die Musik"—"Conversations with Calypso about Music"—written about 1905 and published in 1910 in the Expressionist periodical *Der Sturm*). It has already been mentioned that he took a vivid interest in all important events of the cultural and intellectual life of Berlin. He was in personal touch with many people of the literary avant-garde, especially Herwarth Walden, head of the circle gathered around *Der Sturm,* and his wife, Else Lasker-

Literary Beginnings

Schüler, the prominent poetess. Even from distant Freiburg he followed the doings in Berlin and was in constant touch with Herwarth Walden and his wife. One of his letters, written to Else Lasker-Schüler, is especially noteworthy because it shows that Döblin, the big-city dweller, was by no means unreceptive to impressions from nature—a fact which he was not often ready to admit. The trip to Freiburg, with its frequently changing scenery, had moved him deeply; the "incomprehensible, dark side of this earthly business"[2] had forced itself on him. The letter is even more important as one of the earliest documents of Döblin's religiosity and his inclination toward mysticism. Sitting lonely in his room among his books, he is filled with an awe of supernatural forces demanding veneration:

> It occurs to me that, perhaps, I will become very religious one day. Why shouldn't a spirit knock at the door right now? All the time miracles are happening. When you try to think, everything known becomes unknown. The mystery is just outside the door. I went to High Mass in the Cathedral yesterday. In the afternoon, I went back again alone to the dark empty vault. The best thing we can do is pray. After all, we pray all the time. I find nothing more repulsive than the enlightened liberalism which laughs at religion and considers it opium for the masses.[3]

It is before this background of influences, feelings, convictions, and experiences that Döblin's early writings have to be placed. Among them, the two rather short novels are particularly noteworthy. The first, which bears the title "Jagende Rosse" ("Racing Horses") and is still unpublished, was finished in September, 1900; Döblin wrote it in the last year of high school:

> The novel is dedicated "with love and respect to the departed soul of Hölderlin". (I carried Hölderlin's poetry with me wherever I went.) The title of the novel: "Jagende Rosse." A lyrical first-person narrative. No action at all. Only the course of spiritual development in lyric, metaphorical description. There are no characters other than the "I." In the beginning, the hero lives in youthful, rustic isolation. Then he enters into life, which is described as broadly as the sea. His appetites soon decrease, and the central problem of the book rises to the surface: what is left after the appetites? The hero enters an icy asceticism, a self-submersion in the search for "truth." The goal seems near, but then he sees that he has moved in a circle: his appetites have taken

[35]

on a different cast.—Then decreasing action: his desperation, resignation, finally a frenzied crisis; and then, after weakness and convalescence, the breakthrough to a free life.

This is Döblin's own characterization of the novel.[4] No matter how marked the linguistic and thematic relationship to Neo-Romanticism and to Art Nouveau, it is nonetheless clear how strongly Döblin's own basic theme, i.e., the question of the relationship of the isolated individual to the collective union of nature and life, is sounded. To portray the totality of life even beyond the limits of the socially and psychologically set individual personality is Döblin's most innate desire. This attempt places him in the context of the literary scene around 1900.

The same theme is further developed in the novel *Der schwarze Vorhang. Roman von den Worten und Zufällen* ("The Black Curtain. Novel of Words and Coincidences") which first appeared in installments in *Der Sturm* and in book form in 1919. Döblin set the date of its composition as 1902–1903. Its lyric nucleus is, in the author's words, "the impossibility of the complete union of two people in love. The word 'love' creates the image of such a union, such an inner marriage of beings. Only the isolated, the unconnected, accidental, and lonely being is real and lives; and it encroaches destructively on other lonely things."[5] The novel is easily misunderstood as a depiction of adolescent problems—a topical theme, like that of the whore which Döblin treated in the text "Modern." The themes of love, sexuality, the battle of the sexes, and death always play a decisive role in Döblin's works and in his philosophy of nature. These phenomena pull the individual out of himself into the stream of life. They connect him with the powers of life, the great anonymous, primeval forces which destroy and devour the individual being in order to satiate themselves. The individual hates the sexuality which forces him out of himself, and attempts to protect himself against it:

He could not grasp why man cannot rest fulfilled in himself, why he is split into man and woman, why he is eternally driven beyond his own limits toward other creatures. Everyone bears sexuality's mark of Cain: a fugitive and a vagabond shalt thou be, thou shalt—love. (SV, 41)

Literary Beginnings

The commandment to love, which prevents the individual from remaining proud and at peace with himself is "the command of a pitiless God who hates human pride" (SV, 42).

The *Gymnasium* pupil, Johannes, is "a wordless, isolated person" (SV, 82), for he wants to be alone and does not rely on the apparent certitude which dwells in words. For him, life simmers behind words which cannot encompass its power and complexity. Therefore Johannes despises the "spewers of words"—"*Wortschäumer*"—(SV, 77) who thoughtlessly rely on words. For him there are "no bridges" (SV, 113, 160). Men are windowless, isolated "monads" (SV, 93, 123). But in affirmation of the subtitle "Novel of Words and Coincidences," life outwits him by using the latter for its own purposes. Johannes finally does rely on words and declares his love to his red-haired girl friend Irene:

He was astonished; never had a word of love passed his lips. Tempted, he tried again; the words rolled out calmly and did not collapse under the burden he placed on them. Of their own will one word evoked the next; like that time when he was courting Irene, despising her, and incredulously apologized in secret for himself. . . . As he spoke, the sounds strengthened each other as trumpets strengthen sluggish soldiers and pillars support swaying buildings. (SV, 122)

Language is something suprapersonal, as Döblin repeatedly emphasized in his theoretical writings. Thus life can misuse the illusory possibilities inherent in words and misuse chance events for its own purpose, namely, to sate itself on the destruction of the individual—such is Johannes' belief:

But now I understand the meaning of life. Laughing intentionally in its cruelty and destruction, it aims at annihilation. When one rips the flesh of another being, life is sated, sated through the individual's death. Therefore love is the crown of life. We do not have arms to embrace each other blissfully, but only to protect ourselves, to fight against each other, and to kill—we obliterators of boundaries. Each kiss is a bite mistaken. Alas, for this reason life divides into the duality, man and woman, so that it will attack itself most vehemently and tear itself to pieces. (SV, 153 f.)

For Johannes, sexuality, here representing the power of life itself, is a power which threatens and annihilates the individual. He recognizes the interdependence of all things—an idea central to Döblin's philosophy of nature—but cannot give himself up to that consoling idea because his pride as an individual will not allow him to do so. But his individuality is continuously threatened, for words and coincidences dominate his life: "Chance has extorted my fate from me: instead of me you saw a bugaboo" (SV, 152). In powerless desperation, Johannes defends himself against the forces which shatter his isolation. Consequently, in a scene reminiscent of Kleist's *Penthesilea* he kills Irene and cremates himself with her on a funeral pyre. Out of the flame and ashes, a being arises, who, as so often in Döblin, embodies the irrational power of life, which belittles the individuals it has devoured.

"Jagende Rosse" was a lyrically shaded first-person novel (*Ich-Roman*) whereas *Der schwarze Vorhang* in its third-person naration—which, by the way, is not consistently used—displays a tendency toward greater epic objectivity. The first sentence of the novel betrays Döblin's attempt to establish an ironically detached narrative prose—even in the face of traditional clichés. Whole passages are written in a sober style which merely records events and, in doing so, points toward later works. Döblin's psychiatric interests show themselves in sharply observed and captured pathological scenes written almost in a documentary style: such as *Die beiden Freundinnen und ihr Giftmord*, a criminal case which Döblin described psychiatrically in 1925. Although the novel occasionally slips back into the earlier lack of detachment and the earlier lyricism, it is unmistakable that in language and theme it marks a positive step toward Döblin's ideal of an objective style.

Döblin is rightly regarded as an author of novels and stories; nevertheless, he occasionally made an attempt at working in a different genre. In 1905 he wrote the first of a handful of plays, undoubtedly overvalued if seen as a predecessor of Expressionist drama[6] but very revealing for Döblin's development. This play, performed in 1906 under the pseudonym Alfred Börne in the Residenztheater, together with a play by Scheerbart, bears the curious title *Lydia und Mäxchen. Tiefe Verbeugung* (A Deep Bow) *in einem Akt*.[7]

It is the protest of a play, both written and performed, against its author. The figures and the scenery come alive and make themselves

Literary Beginnings

independent. They speak and act differently from the author's intentions. During the performance, they drive the author and the director from the stage and carry the tamely conceived play insolently and provocatively to a bloody end.[8]

For the poet the inarticulate things are merely dead objects to which he is doing violence by arranging them according to his fantasy. They rebel against this treatment by emancipating themselves and leading their own life. The play, which in many ways anticipates Pirandello's drama *Six Characters in Search of an Author,* is one of the earliest of Döblin's many attacks on materialism.[9] Things have a soul, and man unjustly claims a creative mastery over them.

Yet the play depicts not only the rebellion of the stage properties. The playwright has conceived the two chief characters, Lydia and her knight Max so as to form a medieval couple; he probably wanted to satirize the romanticizing fate-tragedy (*Schicksalstragödie*). Max has journeyed to the Holy Land in order to find the magic flower. It is not the Blue Flower of Romanticism, the expression of sublimated longings, but rather the flower of love's insanity. Astarte, the goddess of conception and fertility, lives in the calyx of the flower. Upon returning, Max meets the funeral procession with Lydia's casket; he kills Lydia's uncle, the leader of the procession, and brings her back to life. At this point, both figures begin to break completely out of the roles prescribed for them by the imagination of the playwright: immortal love makes no appearance, instead we have love-hate and the battle of the sexes—as in *Der schwarze Vorhang.* The two play their roles "until they have shown their natures, these hating, loving beasts, until the icy lovelessness of their love, their scorn of warmth and tenderness, the admission of their 'Phoenician' lust in fighting and murder begins to appear."[10] Brutal sexuality erupts in the figures, and finally even the poet sees himself vanquished by the suprapersonal powers which scoff at his attempt to control and sublimate them. Like Johannes, he, too, says: "Instead of me you saw a bugaboo."[11]

The antagonism of the sexes, which emerges here, also plays an important role in Döblin's novellas. Behind it lies the traumatic experience of Döblin's parents' marriage, and even more so of his own. In some of his novellas, this autobiographical constellation is palpable, most clearly perhaps in "Die Verwandlung," dedicated to Erna Reiss.

Of course, not all of Döblin's novellas were written in the fateful year 1910 or thereafter. Döblin had "gathered the dripping novellas" of the past decade into a volume, *Die Ermordung einer Butterblume*,[12] which appeared in 1913. This collection does not include all of his early sketches and stories; a number of them (such as "Modern," "Erwachen I and II," "Adonis") are missing from this volume and have not yet been published. The chronology of the individual novellas cannot be exactly determined, but if Döblin's own statements are correct, the first novellas in the collection had originated around 1902–1903, contemporaneously with the first short novels. With two exceptions ("Die Memoiren eines Blasierten" ["The Memoirs of a Stuck-up Individual"] and "Das Stiftsfräulein und der Tod" ["The Conventite and Death"] appeared in Albert Richard Meyer's *Lyrische Flugblätter* with woodcut illustrations by Döblin's friend, Ernst Ludwig Kirchner), the novellas were published in *Der Sturm* in 1910 and 1911. The second volume appeared in 1917 under the title *Die Lobensteiner reisen nach Böhmen* ("The People of Lobenstein Travel to Bohemia"). It, too, contains a dozen novellas which Döblin wrote to recuperate from the work on his first long novel, *Die drei Sprünge des Wang-lun*. Several of them were published before 1917 in various magazines. Döblin later used the shorter narrative form less frequently.

Although Döblin's early works have received increasing attention,[13] the novellas clearly stand in the shade of his epic works. Like the complete works of Döblin, they appear at first extremely disparate. Yet most of the stories are thematically and structurally related to a greater degree than one would at first assume. Here, too, Döblin seeks to overcome Neo-Romanticism and Art Nouveau lyricism in favor of a more objective presentation. Irony and satiric bite create detachment. The author visibly tries to achieve a painful exactness and fullness. He turns away from realism, soberly noting, instead, the character's behavior—the doctor-psychiatrist steps into the foreground. Or he fantasizes freely, ending consistently in fairy-tale and parable forms; and, as always with Döblin, the opposite pole is by no means excluded.

What ties most of these novellas to the body of Döblin's work is the thematic foundation developed in the framework of his

Literary Beginnings

philosophy of nature.[14] Many of these novellas portray the intrusion of suprapersonal forces, especially in the form of sexuality, into the protected human sphere. The role sexuality plays for Döblin has been illustrated in the works already discussed. Man "welters in sexuality,"[15] or: "Sexuality wanders dark paths. Man stands in nature's realm and does not escape."[16] But in juxtaposition to this demonic, destructive facet of sexuality stand the gentler forms of love, those which free man from his isolation and incorporate him into the great constellation of nature. Again and again, his characters attempt to break out of their often self-imposed isolation and to regain a greater union with life and nature. This however is frequently only possible in death. The fact that this death is a *Liebestod* in the elements, in the sea, calls to mind Richard Wagner's operas which Döblin greatly admired at that time.

Since not every single novella can be closely examined here, their multifarious character should be illustrated by at least one example, the title story of the first volume of novellas, probably Döblin's best known tale: "Die Ermordung einer Butterblume" which first appeared in *Der Sturm* in 1910. Michael Fischer, the "hero," is the epitome of the meticulously neat philistine who treats his employees sadistically. When walking in the woods, absentmindedly beheading flowers and weeds at the edge of the path, he destroys a buttercup. A little later, in his imagination, he sees himself committing this harmless deed again. The idea of the murder of the buttercup becomes his obsession and signals the disintegration of his personality which was already indicated by neurotic symptoms. The whole forest seems to want to revenge itself on him, and he gets home only with difficulty. He has guilt feelings about his act and at the same time, wants to take revenge on Ellen—the name he has given to the flower—because of these guilt feelings. Reparation can only be made in the framework of his philistine existence as a businessman; thus he opens a bank account for the flower. He plants another buttercup in a pot which he places in his house. When the flower is destroyed by his housekeeper, he feels liberated, has nothing more to do with Ellen, and can kill to his heart's content. Laughing, he disappears into the mountain forest in which he had committed his "evil deed." His mental disturbance has taken a new turn.

The story may have an autobiographical nucleus—the fleeting

affair in Freiburg already mentioned. Whether or not this is the case is an academic question. For surely the meaning of the story does not rest in autobiographical references which, if at all present, are only implicit. Döblin's affinity for psychiatry, whose method of exact description became one of the models for his literary works, is unmistakable. The novella is the precise description of a mental disturbance. Döblin provides a nearly complete catalogue of neuroses which often precede schizophrenia. This preference for the precisely observed clinical symptom often leads to the grotesque in his works. It is tied to the distortion of normal proportions and to the decay of the personality. Grotesque traits are used here in the service of a biting satire on the bourgeois individual.

Yet the more profound reason for Fischer's emerging neurosis is to be found in his distorted relationship to nature. This theme is central to several other Döblin stories, especially those of a fairy-tale character, long before it appeared, monumentally enlarged, in the novel *Berge Meere und Giganten,* among others. Fischer is a city dweller who complains, in his own defense, that the city makes him nervous. He is a man of business and society who, because of his own limitations, can view nature only with the eyes of his petit-bourgeois world. By the very caprice which, he believes, makes him master of nature, nature masters him. Here, too, nature proves itself stronger than man, especially when man does not understand it. Fischer is insensitive to living things; thus in their most inconspicuous form they take revenge on him.

CHAPTER 3

Theory of the Epic and Philosophy of Nature

BEFORE considering Döblin's longer novels more closely, it is necessary to discuss two assumptions underlying the author's art: his theory of the epic and, intimately linked with it, his philosophy of nature.[1] Although the latter began to take clear form only in essays written in the 1920's, it had begun to crystallize, in Döblin's opinion, much earlier, i.e., about 1905. It was at this time, too, that he first engaged in esthetic speculations.

Döblin's epic theory is partly colored by his extraordinarily productive relationship to music and the visual arts. His first efforts in the realm of esthetics were inspired by music ("Gespräche mit Kalypso über die Musik"), but the results remain applicable to literature. Even in later years Döblin repeatedly emphasized the exemplary character of music, especially of symphonic works, for literature.[2] In addition to the insights gained from music, it was particularly the great 1912 exhibition of Futurism in Berlin that helped him further clarify his own position. Gottfried Benn called the publication of the Futurist manifestos "the starting point of modern art in Europe."[3] The most important manifestos, together with a selection of Marinetti's poems, were published in German translation in *Der Sturm*. Döblin, who knew Marinetti's Futuristic novel *Mafarka le futuriste,* also spoke with the Futurist leader when he came to Berlin for the opening of the exhibition. He was profoundly impressed by the pictures and gave the exhibition an enthusiastic review in *Der Sturm.* However, when the deluge of manifestos commenced, he became more critical, and in his efforts to fashion his own style he diverged from Marinetti. But as Armin Arnold has shown, in his novels he remained essentially faithful to the program of the Futurists; indeed, he even attempted to compete with Marinetti's novel.[4] Even *Berlin Alexanderplatz* still reveals how closely the structure of the novel coincides with the structure of Futurist pictures. Regarding this novel, Döblin had often gratefully acknowledged the stimuli of the visual arts which had helped him establish his own position and had strengthened him in insights already gained.

Especially up to his emigration in 1933, Döblin wrote a plethora of essays dealing with art, the role of the artist (writer) in modern society, and, especially, with the structure and function of the novel. His assertions, often made in an insolent and consciously provocative and shocking tone, are not free from contradictions. However, neither these contradictions nor the chronological development of Döblin's ideas concern us here, but only the presentation of those elements necessary for an understanding of his works. These elements are not subject to change but remain constant.

Döblin's attitude was characterized by a dislike for bourgeois art, a dislike which occasionally grew to hatred. His position was strengthened by the influence of the Futurists. His criticism was directed, above all, at the realistic psychological novel. The latter separates the hero from the world, in Döblin's opinion, in order to observe and analyze him precisely as if under a microscope and isolated, as in a chemical or physical experiment:

Carried away by psychological delusions, they have placed, in an extreme way, the isolated man in the center of novels and novellas. They have invented thousands of special, highly exaggerated men in whose complexity their authors basked. Behind this pernicious rationalism the whole world with its multitude of dimensions has disappeared completely. These authors have really worked in a locked room.[5]

This "psychological manner"[6] turns the novelist into a disguised dramatist because he is solely interested in a psychological conflict, isolates the hero from the surrounding world, and thus makes the story untrue. As nearly always, criticism is made in the name of realism, or—as Döblin says—in the name of "naturalism," by which, of course, he did not mean the period concept of literary history. His cry for "naturalism" is coupled with that for totality: no longer should an individual fate be depicted, but rather an event in the whole wealth of its relationships. For this

Theory of the Epic and Philosophy of Nature

reason he prefers to speak about the "epic work" instead of the novel.

At this point, Döblin's philosophy of nature and his theory of the epic converge. His philosophy of nature involves the rejection of the individual in his traditional role and of the cult of great personalities. The individual must let himself go and deliver himself up to the stream of life, to the great forces. At the end of traditional individualism, the individual must disappear from the center of the novel. He must make room for the depiction of the great relationships in which he is embedded. The task of the kind of epic which Döblin describes is to reveal the great movements and events in which the individual is embroiled. Individuality, says Döblin, appears, above all, in women and in the traditional concept of love. For this reason, there are hardly any independent female figures in Döblin's early larger works. He shares this aversion to the sublime eroticism, which is very different from his depiction of sexuality, with Futurism: "Psychologism, eroticism must be swept away: self-denial (*"Entselbstung"*), self-disposal (*"Entäusserung"*) of the author, depersonalization (*"Depersonation"*). The earth must steam again. Away from man!"[7] Later Döblin rejected this radical position as inhuman and, accordingly, modified it.

But what is to replace psychology? The neurologist and psychiatrist Döblin provides the answer: "One should learn from psychiatry, the sole discipline which deals with the whole spiritual man: it has long since recognized the naïve aspect of psychology and limits itself to the notation of processes and motions—with a headshake and a shrugging of the shoulders for the rest and for the 'why' and 'how.'"[8] What Döblin strives for here seems to be a consistent "naturalism" which, by excluding individuality, even that of the author, seeks out the purely objective. This position, reminiscent of Friedrich Spielhagen's theory of the novel—to be understood as militant antisubjectivism and antiindividualism—is strongly mitigated, however, by the role which Döblin assigns to the imagination of the author. Early in his writings, he invented the concept of "factual imagination" (*"Tatsachenphantasie"*) for the synthesis of objectivity and creative imagination.[9] The writer—Döblin consciously avoided the term poet—must know reality, he must be a "naturalist" in Döblin's sense of the word. But then the free play of the imagination takes over: "He [the writer] has to get very close to reality, to its factualness, its blood, its smell, and then he must strike through the thing; that is his specific task."[10] He is not supposed to work mimetically, copying nature, duplicating it—which is impossible anyway—but rather the precisely observed naturalistic details become mosaic stones in the free play of the imagination. In this manner, the work of art creates its own form of reality, a suprareal sphere.

Döblin, in his reflections "on the possibility of an epic style"[11] is striving for the montage technique which he used consistently and successfully in *Berlin Alexanderplatz*. Döblin himself speaks of the "arrangement of the data of reality fixed in word symbols."[12] Such an arrangement results in an "addition to reality: "Literature adds something to the reality, which our daily vocabulary (*"Wortmaterial"*) provides; the data of reality are used to show *that* one adds, *where* one adds, and *what* one adds."[13] In the epic work, the story does not grow from a single point, as in the drama, but from the accumulation of piece on piece. Döblin calls this manner of composition "epic apposition."[14] It is not improbable that here the natural scientist used the crystal as a model. Döblin repeatedly stressed that the individual parts in an epic should be as independent as novellas: "If a novel cannot be cut into ten parts like a worm, so that each part wiggles by itself, it is worthless."[15] However, he did not always avoid the danger which, to the detriment of the unity of the whole, lies in the autonomy of the individual parts.

Since Döblin no longer wants to describe the isolated individual, but the life forces which influence him, he has to place his characters in a multifaceted relation to all areas of life; many things happen to them at the same time. The problem of simultaneity arises for him. Dynamism and simultaneity, the interpenetration of inside and outside, were also characteristic of the Futurist paintings which Döblin admired so much. But Lessing had long ago proven that the visual arts deal with bodies in space, while literature deals with events in time. In literature—as in music—there can only be succession. Yet Döblin has attempted, especially in *Berlin Alexanderplatz*, by means of free association, *style indirect libre*, interior monologue, stream of consciousness, and montage, to give the illusion of simultaneity. Like the Futurists, he demanded speed and dynamics. He advocates a

Theory of the Epic and Philosophy of Nature

"cinematic style" (*"Kinostil"*). This "multitude of visions"[16] must pass by with the greatest conciseness and precision. The influence of the movies on Döblin should also not be underestimated.

The novel, as Döblin conceived it, did not lose its flexibility. On the contrary, it is still the form which can absorb all others: Döblin challenges the epic author "to be decidedly lyrical, dramatic, even reflective."[17] He received linguistic stimulation for the realization of his theory of the epic from the experiments of the *Sturm* circle and from the Futurists, who both tried to find bold new forms of expression. The art of writing—as Döblin saw it—did not consist in a beautiful personal style, but rather in its opposite: "In the absence of the merely beautiful or florid in language, in the avoidance of mannerism."[18] For him, style was something which had to come from the object, not from the aura spread over the object by the author. Consequently, he always stressed the suprapersonal character of language.

The meaning of an epic work did not lie, for him, in the subjective, but in the "elemental attitudes of man" (*"Elementarhaltungen des Menschen"*) which should be exposed. The difference between any invented happening written in the form of a report, merely thought out and written down, and the specifically epic report is "the exemplary character of the event and the figures."[19]

Döblin did not regard art and literature as a personal, self-satisfying game. He was always an opponent of *l'art pour l'art*. On the other hand, he wanted no ties with an ephemeral political or social program, no literature "involved" in this limited sense: "I repeat: the emotion of the writer is in the service, and under the supervision, of knowledge."[20] The writer must humanize and civilize: "He is a particular type of scientist. He is a special alloy of psychologist, philosopher, and observer of society."[21] This perception may, however, no longer serve only a specific social class. Up to now, authors had always produced for basically the same people. Döblin wanted to change this situation: "One must know that the great mass of the so-called lower people now want to, and must, participate."[22] Döblin's rejection of the bourgeoisie and his socialism did not stop at his epic theory and his works, but helped to form them. "Leave the educated, turn to the masses, but first, to this end, turn completely to reality."[23] In his attempt to reach the masses,[24] Döblin, who liked to call himself a proletarian and a worker, was not alone. Brecht, for example, had the same end in mind. Both of them harbored the same mistrust of the art of the bourgeoisie, had the same openness to subliterary traditions, such as the *Bänkelsang* and movies, and often employed a similar didactic tone.

There is no doubt that Döblin was a deeply religious man. Even in his early years his inclination toward metaphysics and mysticism and his attempts to transcend the objective world to reach the total context of existence were evident. Signs of religious emotion recur frequently; witness the previously noted letter to Else Lasker-Schüler, the experience of his trip to Poland, (especially his visit to the Church of St. Mary in Cracow), and the crisis on the flight through France, climaxing in the church at Mende.[25] But even though these experiences seem to point toward his conversion, care must be taken not to read too much Christianity into Döblin at this point. His attitude toward Christianity was actually negative and followed Nietzsche, as the essay "Jenseits von Gott" ("Beyond God") clearly demonstrates.[26] It also shows, however, that Döblin was a seeker and longed profoundly for a new mythology.

Döblin sought to rediscover the great, simple truths in reality, which meant more to him than mere objects (*"Dinglichkeit"*). In this attempt, his concern with natural science was as important as his copious reading. However, in Döblin's view, the natural sciences were caught in specialization and had barricaded themselves behind complicated formulae, so that their findings—such as Einstein's theory of relativity—were intelligible only to the initiated few. Döblin did not want anything complicated, he wanted simplicity, something comprehensible to all. He spoke of the "aberration of the mathematical sciences" and wanted, in contrast, to communicate "a simple and original feeling" (IüN, 16).

Although the two books in which Döblin presented his "system" of natural philosophy, *Das Ich über der Natur* ("The Ego above Nature") and *Unser Dasein* ("Our Existence"), first appeared in 1927 and 1933 respectively, his most important ideas were already present in the early stories and novels. In the bibliography which he added to the volume *Alfred Döblin. Im Buch. Zu Haus. Auf der Strasse* ("Alfred Döblin. In the Book. At Home. In the Street"), he set 1905 as the year in which his interest in natural philosophy awoke. In the twenties, he published a series

Theory of the Epic and Philosophy of Nature

of essays in various magazines, some of which were printed verbatim in *Das Ich über der Natur.*

Döblin assumes that the whole cosmos has a soul. In nature a spiritual, rather than a materialistic, principle reigns. A spirit is operating in it which he calls the "primeval meaning" (*"Ur-Sinn"*) or the "primeval ego" (*"Ur-Ich"*). This primeval ego radiates out of all things, is contained in all things, and joins all things. Consequently, nothing in the world exists in isolation. The spirit is inherent in the things themselves. There is no dualism between spirit and matter. Already in the early, unpublished essay "Qualität und Kausalität," Döblin had formulated his notion that there can be no isolated individual things in the eternally moving continuum.

Nature grows in two directions: toward the simple and toward the differentiated. The simple is found in the form of mass—and that is one of Döblin's most important basic concepts. The beings which exist only in masses (*"Massenwesen"*) are, particularly, the solids, the liquids, the gases and the rays. Their order of importance is explained by the ability of one mass-being to take on the form of another. Of all the mass-beings, water always had the greatest attraction for Döblin. He even wrote a didactic play about it, for which Ernst Toch composed the music. The fact that water is found in all organic beings proves the unity of all life. Even the mass-beings commonly designated as inorganic are by no means dead matter, but have a soul. From them (being great, lasting, and mighty) everything is formed, even man. On the other hand, the differentiated, i.e., the single and complicated form is much less durable, being constantly threatened with disintegration. In nature there is no unformed material, but only transformation. These transformations result from assimilations—an extremely important concept in Döblin's thought. In these assimilations, the world moves onward, but no definite direction of the world-being is evident. Everything—including man—exists only in such assimilations. Thus it is impossible to conceive of organisms as finished, closed forms. They only exist in definite contexts, and these are in flux.

From this sketch of Döblin's ideas there results a consequence important for his art in all—even in formal—respects. The single organism, that is to say, receives its existence and meaning only in connection with the great anonymous mass-beings. An individual being does not and cannot exist by itself: "Factually, the isolation of the individual is strictly insupportable, if only for physical reasons" (IüN, 87). An isolated individual being is untrue and nonexistent. "The personal ego is indefensible. Death permeates the personal ego. Life and truth lie only in anonymity" (IüN, 126).

Since man stems from the anonymity of the (animate) inorganic, from the unrefined and eternal primeval powers which gave birth to, and support, him, he has the instinct to return to them, the drive for depersonalization, for "ego loss"—"*Entichung*"—(IüN, 136). He should be ready to disregard, and even obliterate, his ephemeral ego, sustaining and establishing the bond with anonymity, with the great animate beings instead (IüN, 194). Besides death, in which the final return to the anonymous mass-beings is achieved—prepared for by pain—it is especially love (sexuality) by which man shatters his limits as an individual and sustains his bond with anonymity: "Every being is dominated by its sexuality. But the latter has a suprapersonal character, anonymity" (IüN, 126). For this reason, love, pain, and death are motifs which are seldom absent from Döblin's works.

The awareness of the bond with the great primeval forces awakens in the individual the desire for veneration:

If I were to build a temple, I would place at the center of a court a basin, a large calm water basin. Then I would place uncut stones there. Everyone would be allowed to touch them, to lay his face against them. They would be holy, the representatives of the great spirits from which we, too, derive. (IüN, 151)

The human ego is just as much a part of the primeval ego as everything else, and it is in contact with the inorganic realm—if only by the mere act of eating. Its function is by no means exhausted in this relatively passive role. Döblin distinguishes between four different levels in the human individual, to which he also assigns the name ego—easily a source of confusion. These four egos are: the natural or instinctive ego; the plastic ego, behind which is hidden the centralizing form-impulse, and which roughly corresponds to Goethe's entelechy; the passion ego which integrates the ego into a social order leading the isolated ego to the human mass; and, finally, the private or action ego by which

Theory of the Epic and Philosophy of Nature

the individual closes itself off and opposes the world. The human ego always presents a double aspect: as a part of the primeval ego it is a creature, but as private ego it is simultaneously a creator. It is—as stated later in *Unser Dasein*—"part and counterpart of nature" (UD, 30). This ambivalence in the human individual lies repeatedly at the center of Döblin's works:

That the ego stems from the primeval ego makes it calm and happy *and* makes it restless and unhappy because it is no longer with the primeval ego. Thus all motion in the temporal world is a mutual feeling and seeking of egos seeking to surrender their individuality. In this manner, things touch and transform each other, but—terrible thought—they do not surrender their individuality. Finally, when the struggle is ended—by the death of the individual—things do surrender their individuality. . . . (IüN, 168)

The single thing, by being a carrier of the primeval ego, helps keep the world moving:

The primeval ego—if only in the curvature of time and of isolation—is in every being. As the single thing is not real without the primeval ego, so the primeval ego is not real without the single thing. Thus the single thing acts as agent and creator of the world. (IüN, 244)

These thoughts are expanded and presented more broadly but not differently in *Unser Dasein*; even after Döblin's conversion they were retained. They form the stable element in his thinking. The twofold role of man as "part and counterpart of nature" creates "the dialectic tension" (UD, 176) in which man stands and through which the world moves.

A phenomenon derived from physics—resonance—became more and more important for Döblin. Since everything, even inorganic matter, has a soul, and since the primeval ego radiates from everything, nothing is isolated, but everything is tied to everything else. Resonance becomes the most persuasive proof of this fact, for it is based on the sympathetic vibration of things with equal or similar qualities. It bears witness to the existence of a real connection of man with extrahuman natural forms and with other men, i.e., with society. Indeed only through resonance does the possibility of perception exist. Resonance is a means of forming living beings and masses; it "establishes the Thou in the world." As Döblin puts it, "resonance has a magnetic quality about it. It causes like to find like. At the same time, it is a kind of divining rod, for it reveals similarities; more than that: it strengthens similarities" (UD, 172).

Döblin's philosophy of nature, which has very strong mystic overtones, causing critics to speak of a "godless mysticism"—a term borrowed from Fritz Mauthner[27]—issues in a new image of man and a new view of art. Man is no longer the center of the world; he has ceased to be an isolated individual, but is really imbedded in a collective. The single thing exists only in so far as it takes part in the great stream of life which carries it. It is, to be sure, only the single thing that lives, acts, and seeks to preserve its individual form (principle of individuation). Besides this isolation of all beings there is the union with all things (principle of communion). The resulting dual role has already been noted repeatedly. It leads to an ambivalence of feeling which is clearly evident in all of Döblin's books. As individuals, we feel deserted, and the world seems chaotic to us; but simultaneously, as individuals swimming in the stream of life and borne along by it, we have the feeling of profound security. Even as isolated persons we are still part of the primeval ego and live in communion with everything, especially through the principle of resonance.

Döblin rejected the personality cult. For him, man was not the measure of all things. To him it seemed arrogant to raise the human individual on a pedestal above other beings. From this hubris results—as already demonstrated—the protest of the world of things against man. Every perception began, for him, with the experience of the smallness, insignificance, and impotence of the individual. Every observation can become the starting point for this experience, for example, the crumbling of a dry leaf. But, finally, this depressing feeling leads to the recognition of the wholeness of life:

You are chained to existence—and you exist. You still hold the dry leaf in your hand, crumble it, scatter it: that is me. But already you are trembling: I exist, after all. The feeling runs warmly through you: I am no more than this, but I am. You realize that you are not what you previously thought you were, and very slowly you begin to empathize. (UD, 476)

The great attraction which Buddhism had for Döblin becomes

Theory of the Epic and Philosophy of Nature

understandable: the idea of the *tat wam asi,* of the "that is you," the interdependence, fraternal juxtaposition, and interwovenness of all beings. Man is rooted in nature; this is the consoling thought which preserves him from the impression of chaos and despair: "As a man, even in spirit, even in will I grow no differently from a tree. I want to hang full of apples. Birds shall nest in me. In the winter I want to stand in the snow with larvae between my roots."[28]

CHAPTER 4

*Imagination and Reality—
China and Berlin*

I Die drei Sprünge des Wang-lun

THIS "Chinese novel," as the subtitle reads—the first in the series of epic works—was written under rather unfavorable circumstances. In spite of Döblin's personal and professional problems at that time, it marks the breakthrough not only to a fullscale literary productivity but also to a personal style. This is clearly indicated by Döblin's estrangement from the *Sturm* circle in 1913. Like his future friend, the poet Oskar Loerke, Döblin became more and more keenly aware that his intentions differed in many points from those of the Expressionists, and both rejected, each in his own way, the Expressionistic cult of man. The novel which finally appeared in 1915, after having wandered from publisher to publisher, also made him known to a wider audience; subsequently, Döblin received the Kleist Prize and the Fontane Prize for his novel.

Die drei Sprünge des Wang-lun ("The Three Leaps of Wang-lun") is by no means a Chinese phantasmagoria. Döblin loved facts and factual material and did intensive preparatory work for his novel. He not only gathered an enormous amount of details, but also thoroughly acquainted himself with Chinese philosophy.[1] He shared this preference for Eastern thought and art with many of his contemporaries, nearly all of whom were, to a greater or lesser degree, influenced by the art and philosophy of the Far East. The knowledge of the East was decidedly aided by Richard Wilhelm's translations of Chinese classics into German from 1910 onwards.

Döblin—like Kafka—was particularly fond of the book by Lieh Tzu, to whom the novel is dedicated: in the dedication there is an almost literal quotation from his classical Taoist treatise. Be-

Imagination and Reality—China and Berlin

sides Lieh Tzu, Döblin knew K'ung Fu-Tzu (Confucius)—of whose work he published a selection as late as 1940—[2] the book Chuang-Tzu and, especially, Lao Tzu's *Tao te Ching*, about which he wrote:

> No book can stand beside this one, for it assimilates them all. In a Hegelian manner, it overcomes them not by eliminating or refuting them but by putting them in their place. This book's validity will persist for the next few centuries. The archivists Li Peyang was even wiser than the old Goethe; he rejected all myth.[3]

The theme of the novel—as of all Döblin's novels—is the question of how the individual should relate to his environment. Döblin's experience and his biological and medical research seemed to demonstrate the fragility and impotence of the single being mercilessly trampled by life in its urge to preserve itself. The insignificance of man in the face of an eternal, immense nature (so vividly apparent in Japanese and Chinese color woodcuts) and in the face of suprapersonal powers in general, is one of the basic experiences conveyed by Döblin's works:

> I saw how the world—nature, society—rolls over people, like a heavy tank. Wang-lun, the hero of my first long novel, had this experience. Having survived, he withdraws from this powerful, misanthropic world with a number of similarly wounded friends and challenges it without attacking it. Yet the world rolls over him and his friends.[4]

Wang-lun and his sect want to be weak and to live without resisting Tao, i.e., fate. Paradoxically, however, this very tactic challenges fate, and they are destroyed. Indeed, weakness seems to go against human nature. In an unconditional subjection, man seems to lose his dignity, so that he continually rebels against his fate, only to experience his impotence anew—an endless process.

The narrator begins with the portrayal of the "Truly Weak Ones" who "under the ever passive sky" (Wl, ll) await their final destruction by imperial troops. Then he follows the historical process, the founding and development of the sect and its demise, so that the ending of the novel approximately coincides in time with its beginning. In this sect, an old legend is told in which the basic theme is sounded: the questionableness of human action, which Döblin has already referred to in the dedication. The legend comes from the book *Chuang Tzu*:

Once there was a man who was afraid of his shadow and hated his footprints. To escape them he began to run. The more often he lifted his feet, the more frequently he left footprints. And no matter how quickly he ran, he could not escape his shadow. Then he fancied that he was not trying hard enough and began to run faster, not resting until he exhausted his strength and died. He did not know that he had only to sit in the shade somewhere to be rid of his shadow, that he had only to remain still in order to leave no footprints. (Wl, 13)

The man in the legend hates what he leaves behind him, i.e., his actions. In order to escape them, he flees, which is, in itself, an action. Since by means of action he attempts to escape his action, he finds himself in a vicious circle from which only death can free him. The solution is obvious: be still, and do not act.

Wang-lun, the son of a fisherman from the province of Shantung, is blessed with gigantic stature, extraordinary bodily strength, and uncommon shrewdness—qualities of inestimable value in the brutal fight for existence which he must wage in this miserable environment. It is signally important that he rejects these natural advantages and becomes a Truly Weak One. The poverty and hopelessness of his existence drive him from his home, where the unprotected inhabitants are exposed to every injustice. He goes to the city Tsi-nan-fu, where his life takes a fateful turn. At first he becomes a thief and attempts to steal from a bonze, but the latter outwits him by yielding—a burlesque prelude to the main theme.

The decisive turn in Wang-lun's life is brought about by the murder of his friend, Su-koh, in the open street. After this event, he faces the alternative: rebellion against injustice or acceptance of the unavoidable. At first, he is rebellious. He covers the face of the captain who killed his friend with a mask and strangles him. This strange form of revenge has a symbolic significance: Wang-lun closes his eyes to his own future, i.e., to the necessity of having to travel a new path. "At the same time this movement made him happy and sure: masking. He wanted to close his eyes to the future, which he feared and was ashamed of" (Wl, 74). After this deed, he escapes to the mountains to avoid persecution by the police. His inner unrest cannot be hidden from the beggars and highwaymen he has joined:

They sensed a deep suffering in him, and they considered suffering a

Imagination and Reality—China and Berlin

talent, a gift. The old wisdom of the people filled these lowly people. Not in the men of letters, but in these deserted, much experienced souls flowed the profound basic feeling: "To want to conquer the world by deed is futile. The world is of a spiritual nature, and one should not touch it. He who acts loses it, and he who holds fast loses it. (Wl, 48)

In these last words—a quote from the twenty-ninth chapter of the *Tao te Ching*—the basic thematic concern of the novel—indeed a basic motif of Döblin's entire work, appearing repeatedly in his philosophical musings—is most clearly expressed.[5] The questioning of action is a criticism of the forms of modern life, especially as they have become more prevalent since the beginning of the industrial age. That the common people are in possession of the truth, and that they preserve humanity, is a characteristic trait common to many works of Expressionism. To be sure, this passive attitude repeatedly provokes activity as a necessary counterbalance.

In the Nan-ku mountains, Wang-lun has another fateful encounter: he stumbles on the escaped monk, Ma-noh and in conversation with him and his Buddhas begins to form and develop his own doctrine. Wang, who always seems to do the things that necessity or his inner drive command of him calmly and at one with himself, is quite a different character from Ma-noh. The monk, in contrast, is a religious ecstatic. His ardent desire to fulfill his religious longing for proximity to his gods and goddesses is mixed with the profoundest despair of his ever reaching them. In spite of this, he is filled with pride and arrogance and thus weighed down by shortcomings which reappear in many of Döblin's characters. Pride and arrogance are always based on an overestimation of one's own personality and all too often betray an inner uncertainty. Thus, Ma-noh cannot, as the doctrine demands, obliterate his self.

In the village which the robbers whom Wang has joined attack in icy winter, and in which they settle, Wang formulates his doctrine of nonresistance to fate as he grows into the role of leader. When imperial troops attack them in the village and carry off four of their men, a bitter argument arises over whether they should revenge these brothers. This event becomes a test of their convictions. Wang counters those who agitate for rebellion with a programmatic speech proclaiming the maxims of the Wu-wei, the Truly Weak Ones:

I have heard it on every path, in the fields, streets, mountains, and from the old people that only one thing helps against fate, namely nonresistance. A frog cannot devour a stork. I believe, dear brothers, and want to stick to my belief, that the almighty course of the world is frozen, unchangeable, and does not deviate from its path. If you want to fight, go ahead. You won't change anything; I won't be able to help you. And I will leave you then, dear brothers, for I will cut myself off from those who live in a fever, from those who do not come to their senses. . . . Non-action; be weak and docile like white water, glide like the light off each thin leaf. (Wl, 79 f.)

But this view is untenable. Indeed, it becomes clear that by their passive posture they do not appease fate but provoke it and are finally driven to the killing which they had forsworn. Actually, Wang's very next step shows the impossibility of fulfilling the doctrine of nonresistance. He visits the leaders of the White Water Lily, a powerful secret society, in order to ask for their assistance. He even points out to Chen, the head of the society, that he, Wang, could supply him with an army, since the number of his followers is steadily growing. With the best intentions of protecting his society, Wang betrays its principles, which require living "without resistance to the course of the world" (Wl, 93).

In Wang's absence, Ma-noh takes over the leadership of the society. His pride and arrogance drive him to live up to the doctrine in its greatest purity, but this very ambition keeps him from absorbing the true spirit of the doctrine. He cannot give up his self and feels excluded from the community. It is a new irresistible temptation for him that the mass honor him as a saint. Wang's band disperses, and Ma-noh founds his own band, the Broken Melon. After an attack on the Hill of Women, Holy Prostitution is introduced—that, too, a violation of Wang's rule requiring that "one should not let himself be pushed into the fever of existence by his passions" (Wl, 112). Wang, who, after his return, wears a sword as a symbol of his transformation, reproaches his former teacher for that very thing: his inability to separate himself from his self and from all the joys of life.

But even Wang's conception changes: he lapses into the opposite extreme, no longer feeling able to play the Truly Weak One and believing that he must fight for his brothers. Thus he always lapses from one extreme to the other—a process which only ends with death. When he is captured at Tsi-nan-fu and thrown into prison, he longs for the good fortune of death. He no longer wants to resist, but then he escapes from prison, for even death seems senseless to him. He relapses into his old life as a vagabond, trying to avoid life's painful ups and downs.

Meanwhile, Ma-noh and his society head for disaster. Spurred on by his ambition, the monk tries to achieve the utmost consistency in applying the principle of nonresistance. Very soon, he is facing the same conflict as Wang for the consistently lived doctrine does not lead to an appeasement of fate but to destruction. As Wang had sought help from the White Water Lily, so Ma-noh, too, seeks to meet impending disaster by political measures. He attempts to use a smouldering rebellion as a shield behind which his band can hide unmolested by imperial troops. Here again the law of non-action becomes questionable. Indeed, by using others as means for his own end, Ma-noh violates the humane spirit inherent in the doctrine. Nonetheless, the attempt to save the Broken Melon fails. After a part of his band has been destroyed by the soldiers, he cannot resist the temptation to join the rebellion. He later becomes its leader, even though he secretly laughs at those who are supposed to save his life. His religious ambition, his pride and arrogance remain unbroken. That is also what Wang says of him in retrospect: "He was proud, he was ambitious, he bore arrow, bow, and sword in his heart; he was not a Truly Weak One, not a brother of the glorious Broken Melon. Therefore did I leave him, needing purification and peace for my spirit" (Wl, 261). However, under the impression of his own failure, Wang will later revise his negative judgment of his former teacher, for his contradictory opinions of him are also attributable to his vacillation between rebellion and submission. In contrast, Ma-noh repeatedly lapses into abysmal despair about the insufficiency of his person and his inability to live up to the spirit of the doctrine. Although Wang seeks to move him to dissolve his band in the besieged city, Yang-chou-fu, so that the surviving members will have a chance to save themselves by dispersing, Ma-noh feels that the doctrine demands that he join his brothers and sisters in death. To ease their death,

Wang poisons the fountains of the surrounded city—a terrible decision—reconfirming the earlier experience that it is impossible to live the doctrine of nonresistance and of powerlessness. Again and again, Wang is forced into decisions which violate the principles underlying the doctrine.

The story now turns in epic breath to the events at the court of the Emperor Khien-lung. Döblin always demanded of the novel that its individual parts should have a great measure of independence—like inserted novellas. Thus the third book of the novel has its own meaning far beyond its partial depiction of Wang's adversary who, eventually, must decide the life or death of the Truly Weak Ones. If the Emperor is viewed solely as Wang's antagonist, it is incomprehensible why Döblin devoted so much space to him and his painful decision to repress the sects. In fact, Khien-lung is a much more complex figure. If Wang stands between the extremes of rebellion and submission, the Emperor is caught in the antithesis of humaneness and empire. He has profound insight into the weakness and frailty of man; but he must rule an enormous empire. He is similar, in a sense, to Ferdinand II, the chief character in Döblin's long novel *Wallenstein*. He suffers from the discrepancy between his weak and mortal human nature and the splendor of his imperial dignity. He prefers philosophy and literature to politics; every decision is a burden to him. But he has to decide the fate of the Truly Weak Ones. In order to lighten and share the burden, he has the Tashi-Lama Lobsang Paldan Jische come to advise him. Just as Shen-Te in Brecht's *Good Woman of Sezuan* can only survive as the capitalist monster, Shiu-ta, and thereby create the prerequisite for being good, so the Emperor's position does not allow him to be "pious:"

I am not pious. I had tried hard to think as Your Holiness spoke. It was difficult; one cannot be an Emperor and pious. Let it be. I assure you that it is so. They would have murdered me long ago, if I had been pious in their sense for only half an hour. (Wl, 304)

The gap in his world cannot be bridged. In the long conversation between the Emperor and the religious leader, this dichotomy in the Emperor's attitude becomes evident. For the Lama, he is, first of all, a man who must be concerned about the salvation

Imagination and Reality—China and Berlin

of his soul: "Be the poor little man Khien-lung, the Emperor of the Middle Empire" (Wl, 309). But Khien-lung is the ruler of the largest empire in the world and the son of heaven. To him the members of the sect are rebels who want to put into practice "in a deceitful manner the holy Wu-wei, the nonresistance of Lao-Tzu" (Wl, 310) and thereby threaten to destroy the imperial structure, the political and social order which is always the order of the ruling class. In vain, the Lama presses the Emperor to stop persecuting the sect. Although Khien-lung has sympathy for their situation—and here is the tragic conflict in which he is embroiled—he cannot decide to follow the ideas of the Lama: "A dreadful contradiction. The Emperor sensed that he was nothing, and he had those murdered who sensed it more profoundly, who acknowledged it more deeply" (Wl, 334). He must repress the clear insight into the insignificance of human existence in order to do his duty.

The frailty of the human individual is demonstrated to the Emperor in a staggering way, as the Lama is attacked by the plague and dies a painful death. Döblin does not hesitate to paint in crude pictures the ugly and nauseous sight of death—as Gottfried Benn did in his *Morgue* Poems. Both were, of course, physicians, and the sight of sickness in all its repulsiveness was their daily fare. Sickness closes the Lama's mouth; and in vain the Emperor, in need of advice, awaits an answer. The holy man dies and leaves Khien-lung with his insoluble dilemma. The rage temporarily engendered in the Emperor by the Lama's now being beyond his reach cannot, however, hide the profound despair and perplexity which drive him to suicide. After an aborted attempt to take his own life, he orders—under the influence of his son—the repression of the Truly Weak Ones.

On the other hand, Wang also finds no peace. He tries to draw the consequences from the demise of the Broken Melon by escaping into the bourgeois existence of a fisherman and by marrying. He believes that he has learned that it is senseless to use a sword which only rebounds against one's own chest, and that it is impossible to resist. In the light of this impossibility and of his own failure, Ma-noh's position seems justified in hindsight. But Wang's attempt to live, as it were, in the middle between action and non-action, between rebellion and submission, his attempt to evade the necessary decisions, fails, for he cannot withdraw from his followers.

Once again, he becomes rebellious and asks the White Water Lily for money to arm his brothers. Despite the rebellion against the foreign Manchu dynasty, the natural religion of Wu-wei is still alive in the people, an unquenchable longing for nonresistance and for emersion in the Tao:

> Unnoticeably, like native cress, our houses grow out of the earth, hear the pulses of the spirits and the air currents. Thus we become similar to the Tao, the course of the world, and do not deny ourselves to it. We who have accepted Wang-lun are not tied to fate by shackles and chains. As the old proverbs say: To be weak against fate is the sole triumph of man; we must come to our senses in view of the Tao, and cling to it. Then it will follow like a child. (Wl, 389)

Only by conforming with the Tao can equilibrium, its highest law, be achieved. The Tao embodies all antitheses and resolves them. However, as long as conformity is lacking, every action will evoke a reaction, an endless process of cause and effect.[6] But how can this conformity be achieved? Wang is now convinced that a Truly Weak One can only be suicidal, that he must fight.

Wang is deprived of his seemingly certain victory by a puzzling reversal of fate. The remaining rebels take up a position in the fortified city, Tung-Chong, to await their end. In the cruelty and brutality of war, the doctrine of gentle nonresistance must succumb: Wang himself has a number of subalterns beheaded on the retreat from Peking. Yet it is like a flight from the horrors of war when he almost consciously imitates his youth in Tsi-nan-fu. He "thought of the gentleness of nonresistance and saw himself involved in endless, hopeless murdering" (Wl, 430).

Wang wakes up only when he recognizes, in a robber brought to him for interrogation, his brother and himself. Again the desire rises in him to be poor and passive like the ostracized man, not to resist and to placate fate. Facing the end, he reviews his life. By three leaps over a creek he demonstrates to his friend, Yellow Bell, the decisive changes. The first leap took him out of his youth in the fishing village, and out of what followed, to the Nan-ku mountains, where he met Ma-noh and formulated his doctrine. The second leap returned him to Hia-ho when he was a fisherman and had a wife—in a word, to indifference—but also

Imagination and Reality—China and Berlin

to the following period of his life when he felt urged to take up the sword and rebel against the Emperor. The third leap brought him back to the "correct" side, that of the Nan-ku mountains and the beginning of his doctrine. He has returned to his point of origin. But even though his friend tries to explain, by means of a legend, that they have the correct belief but not the power to translate it into action, Wang demands that he bring his sword. There is fighting to be done: "The time when all travel the pure way has not arrived" (Wl, 470). In spite of the discrepancy between pure doctrine and the impossibility of practicing it, Wang returns to the original point of his maxims:

He remembered the proverbs of Nan-ku: how small man is, he thought, how quickly everything passes away, and how useless protest is. The Imperial and Manchu troops could win, but what use would it be? He who lives in a fever wins countries and loses them; all this means chaos, and nothing more. Wolves and tigers are mean animals. He who takes them as a model eats and is eaten. Man should think as the ground thinks, as the water thinks, as the forests think: without ado, slowly, quietly. They accept all changes and influences, and transform themselves according to them. They who were truly weak toward fate had been forced to fight. The pure doctrine should not be allowed to be expunged and blotted out like bad ink. . . . To be weak, to endure, to submit is the pure way, he thought. To accept the blows of fate is the pure way. Clinging to events, water to water, clinging to rivers, to the land, to the air, always brother and sister, love is the pure way. (Wl, 471)

Again this is a nearly literal quote from Lieh-Tzu. During the night before his destruction by the Imperial troops, Wang meets himself: Wang, passing out weapons to his brothers, sees himself sitting at a table reading. In this vision, the two extremes of his life, the active and passive, resistance and nonresistance, are once again expressed. While the remnants of the Truly Weak Ones fight to their deaths, Hai-tang, the wife of a general, who has lost two children in the fight against the rebels, makes a pilgrimage to the goddess Kuan-yin. The goddess advises her not to rebel against fate, and not to resist. But Hai-tang answers with a question, which concludes the novel: "Can I really be still and not resist?" (Wl, 480)

This is an open ending. It is not only clear that fate cannot be placated by nonresistance, but also that such passivity is contrary to human nature, because human nature repeatedly rebels against the fate imposed on it.

Although Döblin has left no doubt that Wang-lun is central to the novel, an interpretation concentrating on the main figures cannot do complete justice to its complexity. The many interspersed episodes, anecdotes, and parables bear witness not only to the assiduity of the author in collecting material and to his sensibility, but also unfold a picture of Chinese life in the eighteenth century in its totality. The figures of the book live only in a constant reciprocal relationship with the totality of life around them—with the countryside, the climate, society, and its culture. Everything has a place in the novel. The environment in its totality is visible. That Wang-lun is the leader of a mass could create the impression that not the individual but the mass is the "hero" of the novel. Mass scenes in such abundance and in such form—consider the attack on the Hill of Women, the festival which the Broken Melon celebrates on the barque of the goddess Kuan-yin, and the teeming masses of the great cities—were previously rare in the German novel. The influence of Futurism, especially of Marinetti's novel *Mafarka le futuriste,* is clearly evident. However, it is combined with Döblin's sociological and biological views of the insignificance of the single being—another thematic concern of the novel. The truth of existence lies, for him, basically in the masses and in anonymity, to which his heroes often return. When he states in the "Epilog" that, up to his book *Berge Meere und Giganten,* he had hung "on the splendor of the created world and had taken its side," and that with this novel (1924) his preoccupation with "masses and great collective forces, "had come to an end,[7] he is viewing his own development too much from the aspect of the convert concerned with the individual. In *Die drei Sprünge des Wang-lun,* there is no collective hero because Wang-lun, Ma-noh, the Emperor, and their personal conflicts and decisions are too much in the center of the action.[8]

Nonetheless, Döblin—like Kafka—uses no psychology in depicting the "individual" characters. He describes reactions, modes of behavior, moods, and movements, but he almost never intrudes upon the interior of his characters. The plasticity of his language is especially enhanced by this rejection of psychology. In his

Imagination and Reality—China and Berlin

polemics against Marinetti, Döblin had stressed that it was important to deny oneself the use of facile images. Thus he primarily reports and names objects, and the strange and exotic atmosphere of the novel arises less from the rare, unusual or shocking images than from the overabundance of carefully noted details.

Esthetically, the novel is surely a protest against outmoded and, therefore, untrue art forms, but it is much more than that because it depicts, under the guise of a Chinese man from the age of the Manchu dynasty, the dilemma of modern man as Döblin viewed it. Modern man longs to regain the original unity of life and fate, from which he has been ejected, but the dominant powers and systems which want to manifest themselves as forces of fate make such an attitude impossible, because it places their own position in question. Even an open battle against the dominant powers proves to be hopeless.[9] The bitter realization is that one knows the truth but cannot live it. This dilemma recurs repeatedly in Döblin's books.

II Wadzeks Kampf mit der Dampfturbine

Before the outbreak of World War I, Döblin had finished his second major novel, *Wadzeks Kampf mit der Dampfturbine,* ("Wadzek's Battle with the Steam Turbine") which was published only in 1918. This time, he shifted the setting from distant China to his familiar Berlin. His inclination toward exact observation of detail—furthered by his own scientific endeavors and also inherited from Naturalism—and his fascination with factual material[10] led him repeatedly to make detailed studies of his subject. The result was a method of narration that incorporated unintegrated factual material into the novel. In light of this reverence for facts, it is not surprising that Döblin made extensive studies in the Berlin factories of the *Allgemeine Elektrizitätsgesellschaft* (AEG: General Electric) for a novel set in twentieth-century Berlin. He planned a work of several volumes. A "Kampf mit dem Ölmotor" ("Battle with the Diesel Engine") was to be the sequel of the *Kampf mit der Dampfturbine.* This knowledge strengthened the critics in their belief that Döblin's novel deals with man's predicament in the competitive struggle of a capitalist economy and with man's self-alienation caused by the capitalistic economic system.[11] Wadzek, with his steam engines, is pushed into the background by the steam turbines of his opponent, Rommel. He is overpowered by technological progress, and he, the man who defended himself with might and main against destruction, is marked as a helpless and powerless cretin. In his battle against Rommel, Wadzek finds an ally in Rommel's engineer Schneemann (!). With every means at his disposal—in part even with illegal machinations—he attempts to stave off his fate, but all in vain. His fear of the loss of the basis of his existence results in inner strife and disjointedness in his life, in compulsion, and in aimless walks and rides through Berlin. Certain traits of Döblin's narrative technique reminiscent of *Berlin Alexanderplatz*—simultaneity, changing perspective, and psychic automatism—can be explained by the material and theme.

To this onset of a story that could as easily have been developed tragically, Döblin gave a grotesque twist. He gave the battle of the two "heroes" a larger dimension. Wadzek and Schneemann are no longer merely battling against the technological progress which makes their steam engines obsolete in comparison with Rommel's steam turbines, but see themselves as champions of individual freedom, of man himself, against oppression by Rommel and his ilk. Thus a revolutionary metaphor is introduced which continually underlines the discrepancy between reality and the imaginary world of Wadzek and Schneemann. The novel achieves its comic, ironic, and grotesque effects because of this intellectual contrast between mind and matter. The revolutionary pathos which carries Wadzek away is completely unsuited to the actual situation. Note the following address to his partner Schneemann: "Wadzek yelled hoarsely: 'Are you my comrade-in-arms? We will stand with bared chests, without barricades, when the storm breaks'" (WaK, 33). By assuming the role of a revolutionary which does not at all fit the given situation he tries, by overcompensating in this way, to overcome the shock of loss.[12]

Because Wadzek cannot avoid the bankruptcy of his factory—Rommel buys up his promissory notes—he retreats with his wife, his daughter and Schneemann to his summer house in Reinickendorf, in order to defend himself and "to affront" the whole world (WaK, 92). The discrepancy between the pose of the conspirators and the real situation leads to more grotesque misunderstandings; for Wadzek transforms his summer house into a fortress with guards and alarm devices and longingly waits for

Imagination and Reality—China and Berlin

the attack of the "enemies" from Rommel's camp. A former doorkeeper's wife supplies him with daily provisions. When, one day, her young son brings the food, Wadzek sees in him an enemy and inundates him with a torrent of abuse—completely ignoring the situation and the boy's explanations. This exposes his rage, his hatred, and his animosity, but also the prejudice unleashed in him by the sudden blow of fate and by the concomitant uprooting.

The "Siege of Reinickendorf" finally ends with Wadzek, who believes that the opposition has started the attack, shooting at harmless bird poachers pursuing their illegal trade on his grounds. Wadzek and Schneemann are arrested by the police after Schneemann, on Wadzek's orders, has unsuccessfully tried to ignite dynamite planted in the basement.

At the police station, Wadzek thinks that he will be able to epitomize his role as martyr. He is convinced that he has killed one of his enemies—if not Rommel himself—on his grounds. In vain he asks to be booked for murder. Of course, these demands are completely incomprehensible to the officers, who believe that the two are drunk. But, following the insane logic of his ideas, Wadzek sees in this misunderstanding by the officers only a particularly mean way to silence them. He is left with no alternative but to return home.

Now he becomes the true and caring family man. His newly awakened love for his thoroughly ugly, monstrous, and primitive wife brings only a new bitter disappointment, however. For the wife, formerly completely dominated by Wadzek, is rehabilitated and uses her newly gained freedom for drinking bouts with dubious female companions. Wadzek witnesses a grotesque orgy in his own house, in which his wife's drives, previously hidden under the dark cloak of bourgeois propriety, become evident. Repulsed, Wadzek moves into a hotel.

Even his attempts to hold free lectures at a polytechnical school about his newly gained insights meet with no success. After failing in his profession, he also fails in his efforts to establish a new position in his family and to find a new profession which would put him back on his feet. This twofold failure in his profession and in his family makes him want to escape: he flees with Rommel's girl friend Gabriele, the pliant, adaptable, motherly contrast figure whom he had once rescued from the streets.

She had returned to him when Rommel had refused to help. They escape to America on a turbine-driven ship—leaving the family behind, like Döblin's father.

In Wadzek's story, Döblin anticipated the fate of many members of the German middle class. Because of technological innovations and later because of the inflation, many experienced the collapse of their professional existence. The concomitant loss of authority in the family tempted many to flee from this unbearable reality.[13] While the social components of the novel should not be underestimated, this theme is not sufficient to account for the whole novel in its satiric, ironic, and burlesque aspects. It should rather be viewed in relation to *Die drei Sprünge des Wang-lun*. Döblin himself referred to the connection in the "Epilog":

I had to pursue these things farther. I did not want to be chained to ponderous and dark things. I did an about-face and was unintentionally, indeed completely against my will, drawn into light, fresh, and burlesque things.[14]

These "things" which Döblin mentions here are basic to *Wang-lun*, the antithesis of submission to, or rebellion against, an overpowering fate. A careful study of *Wadzek* shows that Döblin is playing ironically with the problems of *Wang-lun*. Both positions—revolt against fate and appeasement of fate by submission—are presented with ironic detachment.[15] One half of the novel, up to and including the "Siege of Reinickendorf," shows Wadzek's rebellion against his fate—the ruin of his steam engine factory. It has been seen how, by means of exaggeration, the narrator gives this protest an impotent as well as grotesque quality.

In the second part of the novel, the transformation characteristic of all of Döblin's heroes occurs: Wadzek recognizes the hubris of his protest, the overestimation of his own person, and is ready to place himself in larger contexts and to acknowledge the interdependence of all things and events. But the circumstances—Wadzek's lectures to a wife who usually sleeps right through them and a daughter who bothers him with carefully interpolated questions—as well as his choice of examples cast an ironic light on his insights.

Imagination and Reality—China and Berlin

Maneuverability, adaptability, and assimilation to the ever changing situation—concepts which, as *Das Ich über der Natur* demonstrates, are central to Döblin's thought—are raised here to the principle of life, in an ironic fashion, admittedly. Unconditional retention of a position and rigidity in the face of life's flux are rejected:

> Stability: that is false praise. If I were noble, I would incorporate a weather vane into my coat of arms. The principle of adaptability is the most important; one must renew oneself. One must have the ability and courage to follow the times, the events, the men, like a weather vane or any light object. (WaK, 375 f.)

This brings to mind the following sentence from *Wang-lun*: "Be weak and docile like calm water; glance off of every thin leaf like the light" (Wl, 80). But the ironic tone is always present in *Wadzek*. Correspondingly, Wadzek's concept of heroes and heroics changes. In the first part, he sees himself as a heroic champion of the freedom of all men against Rommel's oppression and as a martyr. In the second part, he considers his own "heroic" resistance to fate skeptically and ironically. He tells Gaby, Rommel's lover, about his daughter's evening at the theater and explains his ideas about heroics to her:

> The hero is always unable . . . to do something without apparently breaking his heart, so to speak. . . . What does a child like Herta learn from Macbeth? I no longer know the play very well; but, surely, she convinces herself that it is good to be such a type, or not to be deterred from one's plans. Right through. Straight through. And then howling. Applause for the tragic character. Flexibility is much more important. I, for example, would depict a strong man, very muscular, a real athlete who can hardly move because of his strength. Then a puny little kid, a Tom Thumb, would cut through a sinew from behind, as with a horse. Then they would see what fat heroics are all about. . . .
> Odysseus is more important than Achilles or Hercules. If Achilles had not been killed at Troy, he would have died on the way home; he would not have found his way home like Odysseus. What is the use of heroics? (WaK, 377 f.)

Finally Wadzek flees with Gaby. After he is ready to deny his self, he can really approach Gaby, who has waited to devote herself to him. But even this happy ending dissolves ironically.

CHAPTER 5

History and Science Fiction

I Wallenstein

DÖBLIN'S next novel, written during the First World War, again turned to quite different times and settings, namely to the Thirty Year's War. "Then the War came. I floated around Alsace-Lorraine. Halfway through 1916 I buried myself in *Wallenstein*. I wrote in great peace, pausing for months because of illness; finished at the end of 1918."[1] The novel finally appeared in two volumes in 1920.

As with his other two novels, Döblin had made preliminary studies and had integrated an enormous amount of factual material into his work. Günter Grass has justly called these masses of narrative material an "epic design" ("epischer Aufriss").[2] Although the novel is entitled *Wallenstein*, the Emperor Ferdinand II is at least of equal importance with the great general; and Wallenstein is his contrast figure:

The book should really be called 'Ferdinand the Other.' . . . But Wallenstein embodied the era and the circumstances. . . . Ferdinand the Other, the Emperor (whom I had to create) is placed in a conversation with the almighty facts. He answers the thunder. Result? He gives up. That was how I saw things then. Like Wang-lun, Ferdinand succumbed to the "world."[3]

In his retrospective view as a convert, Döblin apparently wanted to make us believe that this was a "historical" novel with no links to the present. Yet in the essay "Der historische Roman und wir,"[4] he explained that, for him, this kind of novel could not exist because "historians want something from history."[5] While the historian honors a "fancied ideal of objectivity,"[6] the writer, in free manipulation of the elements of reality, constructs the apparent reality of the novel. Through resonance—an extremely important concept in Döblin's thought—an affinity between the author and a particular historical period is established. During the process of writing, the transition from the borrowed and imagined tradition "to a genuine, that is, to a purposeful and emotionally fraught reality" takes place.[7] But since the author is not only a private person, but also a representative of his age, this identification between the author and his material has yet another meaning: "For if the author is an open and complete man, he does not undertake a private altercation with his chosen material but implants the fire of a present situation in the past era."[8]

It should be clear by now that Döblin's choice of material was by no means arbitrary, especially if one's view is directed away from the Emperor, a basically apolitical person who sinks into an ever increasing mysticism, and toward Wallenstein. From this perspective, the war and the preparations for it appear as an enormous capitalistic enterprise—one need not look long for parallels in the twentieth century. But, beyond that, Wallenstein stands at the crossroads of German history:

A man like Wallenstein should have accomplished something. He was about to undermine the independence of the princes. The wars gave him the pretext for his army and for the extremely effective forced contribution system. Then he was defeated, and Germany with him: the independence of the princes was victorious, and the German subject was born.[9]

Wallenstein had the opportunity to smash feudalism, as Richelieu did concurrently in France. But he did not grasp it and the consequences were, in Döblin's opinion, still visible almost three centuries later, as the roar of cannon reached his ears from Verdun. For he viewed World War I and its consequences in the light of an everlasting struggle against feudalism.[10]

Döblin's novel encompasses the time between the Battle at the White Mountain near Prague (1620) and the assassination of Wallenstein (1634) which, in the novel, coincides with the death of the Emperor Ferdinand—an historical inaccuracy because the Emperor died in 1637. Although Döblin unfolds the whole gigantic panorama of the war before our eyes, Wallenstein, and even more so Ferdinand, are the dominant figures. Other characters, such as the king of Sweden, Gustavus Adolphus (who, visualized as sailing innumerable ships across the Baltic Sea, provided

Döblin with the initial stimulus for his novel)[11] are overshadowed by these two mighty protagonists. While Wallenstein devours himself in restless activities and finally becomes the victim of his own contradictory and muddled plans, Ferdinand detaches himself increasingly from his throne and his occupation. He withdraws from politics, sinks mysteriously within himself, and returns to the mystic union of all being. Thus here again the theme of *Wang-lun* is sounded: the questioning of the possibility and meaning of human action, the antithesis of passivity and activity, resistance and nonresistance—now no longer centered in one person but juxtaposed in the two dominant figures. According to Döblin's own interpretation, Ferdinand chooses this path because he feels sated; and in the end he casts off everything. But, in addition, there are always signs of Ferdinand's boredom with the never-ending intrigues at court, with the endless maneuverings of the political powers—schemes and intrigues which do not bring the desired peace.

The novel begins after the defeat of the Protestants by the Catholic League led by the Bavarian Elector Maximilian. This victory contains the seeds of a new conflict. For the proud, ambitious, and power-hungry Bavarian prince lays claim to the lands of the exiled and outlawed king Friedrich von der Pfalz (Frederick of the Palatinate) and to his electoral power. If he gets what he wants, the precarious balance of power in the Empire will be tipped in favor of the Bavarian ruler, possibly even endangering the Hapsburgs. Ferdinand's advisors clearly foresee the rekindling of the war and the entrance of the Protestant powers, England and Denmark, into the war. The decision rests squarely with the vacillating Emperor, whose imperial sense of justice demands of him that he grant the Bavarian prince his wish for having carried the burden of the war almost singlehanded. However, he attempts to prevent an increase in power for the prince by writing secret letters to the English ambassador.

Like the Emperor Khien-lung, Ferdinand is neither equal to the conflict of feelings and ideas nor to the intrigues. Even here his inclination "to avoid difficulties by flight" (Wa, 628) is evident. He wants to withdraw from the power struggle as soon as he has placed his son on the throne. His desire to abdicate is strengthened by the victories of the League's armies over Ernst von Mansfeld and Christian von Halberstadt, two Protestant

History and Science Fiction

leaders. That means not only another increase in power for his brother-in-law, Maximilian, but also a new humiliation for himself. For, on Maximilian's insistence, he had refused to accept his rightful leadership of the League. All of this has strengthened in him the wish to withdraw, to leave the throne to a stronger man, and to sacrifice himself. Indeed, he goes so far as to reproach his advisors for not having removed him from power. The high concept he has of the imperial office—the position of maintaining the balance of justice over the parties—cannot be put into action: Ferdinand must repeatedly experience being drawn into the politics and intrigues of the day—and having his rulership conflict with the partisan politics of the various princes and factions of his own house. Because he occupies the highest position, he feels his impotence so much more strongly. Because he is not removed, he must make the decision: he enfeoffs Maximilian, thus kindling the war anew.

In the meantime, in besieged Bohemia Wallenstein's hour is approaching. Brutally and with extreme persistence, not stopping at treachery, deceit, and extortion, and with the help of confederates (among them the Jewish banker Bassewi), he has amassed a huge fortune in the shortest time, especially by leasing Prague's mint and by an incredible currency swindle. In *Der deutsche Maskenball*, Döblin described Wallenstein as a

> character . . . , who never wavered, always knew where his advantage lay—and, truly, where the advantage of the German anti-prince faction lay—who applied his powers mercilessly, lightninglike in the most advantageous place. The reflexlike certainty of his nature, his cold clearness—his rage, his mocking personality, greed, and nobility.[12]

In his efforts to amass more and more power and wealth in his hands, men become for him merely tools of his will. Once they are no longer useful to him, he ruthlessly disposes of them. Wallenstein acknowledges "nothing but power" (Wa, 231). "Friedland acknowledged only the gamble in which the pressure grew with the size of the wager. He knew only how to dispose of things or overthrow them, but not how to hold on to them. He was only the force that caused solids to liquefy. He shuddered and gnashed his teeth when something solid opposed him" (Wa, 374).

Ferdinand the Other almost always has a peculiar vision when he meets Wallenstein or thinks about him: he feels as if a giant centipede were running across him. The image suggests that Wallenstein is Schopenhauer's blind will of life itself.[13] Ferdinand is subjected to him as long as he has not rid himself of his self and of his own claim to power. Thus it is expressly stated after he has let himself go: "He looked up, no centipede, no repulsive stomach over him" (Wa, 699). Because Wallenstein and other figures of his type embody this blind, urgent irrational power of life, he, Tilly, and Maximilian are occasionally metaphorically described as animals, while Ferdinand who, in these surroundings, is the "Other," is often described as a child, and the childlike side of his being is frequently stressed.

On the one hand, Wallenstein becomes involved in ever greater undertakings, and on the other Ferdinand sinks into ever greater passivity. Wallenstein offers the Emperor an entire army which he wants to garrison on imperial lands. Ruthlessly he defends the Emperor's absolute right of confiscation, which gives the Emperor ownership not only of the lands but also of the people on them. And everything must be at his disposal in time of need. With brutal persistence Wallenstein sticks to the principle that the war must feed the war.

Earlier, he had offered Maximilian a similar deal but had been refused. This proves that Wallenstein was not concerned with overthrowing the throne, but with gaining the key position in the Empire for himself. When he later sees that he can no longer rely on the vacillating Emperor, he deals with all other parties in order, if necessary, to join them in war against the Emperor. Similarly, religious grounds play no role in the "religious" war. For him, power and force are areligious; they are a law unto themselves and use religion at most for their own purposes.

Because Wallenstein's offer provides the Emperor with an opportunity to chill Maximilian's hunger for power, he accepts it. Ferdinand is fascinated by power; he "felt with an unclear joy that he was trusting the Bohemian in a way, and with a strange urgency, as no man before him, perhaps as a wife trusts her husband" (Wa, 223). But he is just as strongly repelled by the power —and the politics which force him to condone such measures in order to defeat the Protestants, to preserve his own house, and to achieve the tardy peace. He realizes more and

History and Science Fiction

more what terrible power, he, the protector and propagator of the Empire, has delivered himself up to. Wallenstein wants to station himself and his unruly army within the Empire in order to stamp out all resistance. The Emperor realizes that "it is hard, it is unnatural, it is the planned destruction of whole lives, whole countrysides created by God" (Wa, 267). But he cannot carry out his decision or dismiss Wallenstein because his court demonstrates to him that he needs the general. Resigned, he says to the Empress after the discussion with members of the court: "It is difficult for me. It has something—unbearable for me. Too much so, Eleonore" (Wa, 270).

Wallenstein, for his part, continues to arm and advances, in "the terrifying consequences of action" (Wa, 304), from success to success; for he wants to set up a military dictatorship over the Empire. After several victories over the Danish King Christian, he reaches the sea. He also becomes the Duke of Mecklenburg. But the climax of his career is simultaneously its turning point, as he cannot conquer Stralsund by siege. It must have been symbolic for Döblin that the sea was fatal for Wallenstein. For water was for him not only one of the basic elements, but also the symbol of life itself; indeed, it was exemplary for the proper attitude toward life: nonresistance and adaptability. Water lies outside of Wallenstein's power, which, as we have seen, destroys solids.

The conquest of North Germany presents the Emperor with new problems. The Pope urges him to restore Protestant convents to Catholic hands. The signing of the Edict of Restitution causes the war to continue, although the Emperor always hopes to end it—not only in Germany but also in northern Italy.

At this point, faced with an insoluble dilemma, Ferdinand begins to retire more frequently to his hunting lodge in Wolkersdorf, surrounded by woods, which is an external expression of his internal withdrawal. He sees his house blessed anew by the successes in North Germany and in Mantua. He now wants to have his son Ferdinand crowned Roman King, but needs the approval of the Electors. The latter, however, will only agree if Wallenstein, the most powerful man in the Empire, is dismissed. The general, having gathered his troops near Regensburg, site of the voting, reminds the Emperor that they are at his disposal. But when Ferdinand plays Wallenstein off against the princes, the old imperial structure is ruptured—an act that has grave consequences.

The decision lies completely and wholly with the Emperor, and, as he points out to his confessor, Lamormain, he could make it dependent on an accident. In Döblin's interpretation, this is the moment of greatest power; but, simultaneously, in the Emperor's idea of letting accident play a role there lies the resigned insight that it makes no difference what he does, that in the end things— in spite of his power, his maneuvering, his directing—are out of his control. Although he sees the situation and the meaning of his decision clearly, he is indifferent. Nowhere is it more evident how unpolitical and withdrawn from the world he already is. Responsibility, action, guilt, and sin are things without meaning to him. He follows the way to mysticism more and more consistently.[14] Under the influence of Lamormain, he finally dismisses Wallenstein.

But then Sweden enters the war as a new party, the imperial general Tilly suffers a humiliating defeat near Breitenfeld, and after the recently conquered North Germany has to be surrendered, the Emperor urges the recall of Wallenstein. During the audience, the indifferent, silent Emperor thinks about the necessity of having such men of power: "Perhaps one should put such men on the throne; that would be the most correct, the easiest thing" (Wa, 565). A similar wish stands at the beginning of the novel, namely to give way to Maximilian as the stronger man. While Wallenstein begins to rearm like "a megalomaniac" (Wa, 575) and forges grandiose schemes, Ferdinand withdraws increasingly. He wears the clothes of a simple workman—that, too, an external sign of his internal transformation. More and more often he goes to Wolkersdorf, and his extended walks in the woods last longer and longer. Mystically, he sinks into powerlessness as he achieves unity within himself. "In a mysterious way" (Wa, 586), he retreats within himself, shuts himself off from the outside world, and thus begins his growth toward spiritual freedom and innocence.

This process is by no means completed without moody and tormenting vacillation; sometimes the Emperor convulsively tries to find his way back to power. But with growing certainty he sees his way, which his confessor, Lamormain, also clearly foreshadows: ". . . like one blessed, the Emperor laid all power

History and Science Fiction

aside, exposed its weakness and its pettiness" (Wa, 629).

Wallenstein's betrayal and the plan of the court to remove him for political reasons provide the final stimulus for pursuing the path to the end. While Wallenstein is murdered in Eger, "sucked up again by the dark forces" (Wa, 720), Ferdinand the Other joins the wandering, suffering masses of the great war. When finally he meets the miserable wooden casket of his general, he surrenders completely. He relates:

> He had been in a high office, had given it up. For ruling had little purpose. Everything runs by itself. Everything runs by itself. He had also realized that it is all for the good, one only had to understand how. (Wa, 732)

When, at the end of the war, Döblin brought *Wallenstein* home without a closing chapter, he was "deeply impressed by the sight of several black tree stumps along the street. "The Emperor Ferdinand, has to go there, I thought."[15] Thus Ferdinand the Other returns to the forest where he befriends a goulish creature which eventually kills him. As Wallenstein had found his way back to the "dark forces," so he, too, finds his way back to nature, which, in Döblin, is so frequently symbolized by forests and by this creature.

The war shows not only the vulnerability of man, "the vacillation of all human relationships" (Wa, 629), but also exposes in Ferdinand the impotence of those in power. Wallenstein finds no peace in his blind activity and greed, while the Emperor gains increasing detachment and lays down his power. Like the figures in Büchner's drama *Dantons Tod,* he sees the fatalism of history which, obeying its own laws, steps over the very people who think they are directing it. Thus the novel ends with a future vision of the terrible, self-perpetuating war.

Here, too, only a few of the individual figures and events from the complex panorama can be discussed. The Emperor, Wallenstein, and all the other figures are imbedded in their age and stand in a continual reciprocal relation with the events. The intrigues at court, the generals and diplomats, the princes and bishops, are all part of the portrait out of which the main actors step. Often the plethora of events can only be conjured up in a juxtaposition of catchwords. And here again Döblin is fascinated by the masses, the armies, the refugees, a trait which is further magnified in his next novel.

II Berge Meere und Giganten

Döblin's career as a writer offers many dramatic interludes. In 1920, he published *Lusitania*,[16] a play which uses the torpedoing of the ship by that name solely as a point of departure. The drowned people are taken by sea creatures to the empire of a legendary king of the bottom of the sea and are finally condemned to return to the land. They feel guilty and want to be saved by the old king. After they have returned to the land, they meet a figure which symbolizes conscience. Each recognizes in it someone he or she has sinned against. They beg this figure, which urges them to pray, for forgiveness and salvation.

The play *Die Nonnen von Kemnade,* which had its premiere in 1920, also deals with salvation. Before Döblin began working on *Wallenstein,* he had planned to depict the fall of Byzantium. But then his work on *Wallenstein* pushed everything else aside. When in 1920 he renewed his interest in the old idea, he happened upon the subject in one of the yearbooks of German history.[17] Here again the well-known motif of the battle of the sexes appears. But in the center of the action lie the religious dialectics of sinless world piety and ascetic seclusion and longing for the next world. The abbess, Judith, has the traits of natural sensuality and an orgiastic love of life which earns her the accusation of incontinence from the ecclesiastical hierarchy and the persecution of the religious fanatic, Ambrose. On the other hand, she wants to be delivered from this life. She accepts her nature and herself but also longs to leave her life behind her. The play is not only a new proof of how important religious problems are for Döblin, but especially of how important the constant dialectic of self-assertion and self-denial are in his work. The Knight Templar whom Judith meets in prison preaches the "low God," a pantheistic religion:

Worship when I uncover the stone. It is youth with the soul of a man and of a woman, the low God. He is in you. When he leaves you, you will be dead. He is in all of us, in the animals, the trees, the air. You must embrace him.[18]

History and Science Fiction

The same feeling of veneration for what Döblin calls the "low God"—representing supranatural forces—prevails at the end of *Berge Meere und Giganten* ("Mountains Seas and Giants").

Having held a mirror up to the Great War of his age, it is no surprise that Döblin should now write a "science fiction" novel, thus moving from the realm of history to that of prognostication. The novel is not utopian in that Döblin created no picture of an ideal world, but only attempted to describe the developments and events of the future by poetic means.

Döblin often thought about how the future would look and repeatedly attempted to sketch it. Thus, for example, in *Der deutsche Maskenball,* the dominant tendency of the age is seen as intensive industrialization, before which all differentiation becomes irrelevant. The characteristics of the coming age are the massing of mankind, the possibility of battles of the masses, the oppression of weaker groups, and the accumulation of power in the hands of the few. This will bring about the end of the industrial movement and, with it, the enervation of the technological-industrial complex. The leading role will be assigned to another group of ideas. In many respects, industry will become superfluous: "Moving the technological complex into the background will make way for a comprehensive cultural movement. Only then will there be a greater cultural production."[19] This evolutionary historical outline reappears in *Berge Meere und Giganten.*

In an important essay, "Der Geist des naturalistischen Zeitalters" ("The Spirit of the Naturalistic Age"), Döblin again tried to analyze his own time and to forecast the tendencies of the future.[20] He states that in the Middle Ages, all human existence was directed toward another world. The elemental feeling of this era was the feeling of one's own insignificance, but also that of metaphysical pride. The science of this age was the science of the other world, i.e., theology. The ever growing inclination to observe this world, which theology thought irrelevant led to a turning point. The power which supplants transcendental knowledge is the naturalistic spirit. It becomes especially evident with the appearance of technology in the middle of the nineteenth century. Biologically, this new naturalistic spirit is a "special attitude of groups of people under the influence of society's drives."[21] Like every culture, the naturalistic one is a fleeting

[79]

attempt of the collective being to change itself. For the consequent variety, strong men who are the first to change and show variation are the measure.

On the basis of this historical outline, Döblin attempts to understand his epoch in all of its manifestations and to characterize it more precisely. The people of this age are moved by a contradictory feeling: on the one hand, they have an insight into the irrelevance of the single human animal, its loss of the central position in the world, and a feeling of smallness; but on the other hand, they have a feeling of freedom and independence, which arises from the certainty of not having to live for the next world and of having to accomplish everything oneself. From this awareness grows a drive for the most forceful activity, which finds expression in the permanent technological conquest of the world. It is important to keep in mind that Döblin always sees an intellectual power behind material changes, in this case the spirit of the naturalistic age.

This power is especially evident in the large metropolitan areas and in the mass populations. The big cities "are the coral reef for the collective being, man."[22] Monotony and uniformity are further characteristics of the age. The human group tries to degrade its members to specialists, a process resulting everywhere in battles between the whole individual and the drives of the group to make him a bearer of a specific function. The lust for space and for expansion is another expression of the naturalistic spirit, which leads to wars. The common enemy of this movement, which is more or less identical in Communism and Capitalism, is the antinaturalist and humanist, as Döblin saw him embodied in Tolstoy. Obviously under the influence of the naturalistic spirit, social concepts, such as the family, morality, as well as art, had to change, a fact clearly demonstrated by Döblin's entire work.

It will have become evident that Döblin has here gone beyond mere analysis of the present. In *Berge Meere und Giganten* he, rather, depicts the expansion of the naturalistic spirit up to its inevitable turning point in magnificent images. But how does this epoch end? Old traditions and concepts (the earth, race, blood, religion, and mysticism), from which countermovements arise, lie beneath the surface. This turn to mysticism, which always enters in Döblin's works when perception, knowledge, and tech-

History and Science Fiction

nology have reached their limits, is extraordinarily characteristic of him. "In the first segment of this period, nature is merely unknown and is studied passionately; later it becomes a mystery. To feel the mystery and to express it in its own way is the great task of this period."[23]

Döblin wants to portray "the development of our industrial world until about the year 2500," "a completely realistic and at the same time, completely fantastic thing; Jules Verne will turn in his grave—, but I intend something quite different from him."[24] The question which interests Döblin is: "What will become of man if he continues to live in this way?"[25] Technology increases the possibilities of man to an incredible point, but it leads almost to self-destruction; as in Goethe's "Zauberlehrling," man cannot contain the forces he has unleashed, and nature proves stronger than man:

> In a book transcending time and space I could tell of the development and misuse of technology to the point where it becomes a biological exercise, effects changes in man who himself was the originator of the development, and how it leads man back to the cretaceous period. Terrified, the remainder of mankind falls on its knees and makes humble sacrifices to the primeval powers.[26]

Thus the novel expresses anew Döblin's basic dichotomy: "human power against the power of nature, and the impotence of human power."[27]

In the essay "Bemerkungen zu *Berge Meere und Giganten*," Döblin also sketched the long history of the origin of this work and gave several explanations which contribute to an understanding of the book. After extensive studies in history and politics, he had been strangely touched by the sight of stones on the Baltic Sea. That led to a renewed preoccupation with nature, scientifically and especially philosophically in the essays "Das Wasser," "Die Natur und ihre Seelen," and "Buddha und die Natur," which were later embodied, in part verbatim, in his philosophical essay *Das Ich über der Natur*. The upshot of his scientific studies, especially the study of biology, geology, and mineralogy, was a comprehensive collection of materials. The description of these facts in the novel is, as always, by no means an end in itself, but is, as the "Dedication" makes particularly clear, "a mollifying and solemnizing song to the great maternal forces."[28] For the purpose of Döblin's book in the framework of his natural philosophy was "to praise the world being."[29] Only in this way can the many digressions be explained; and Döblin is often in danger of giving in to the inherent tendency of these episodes to become autonomous and thus destroying the unity of the whole.

To an even greater degree than Döblin's other long novels, *Berge Meere und Giganten* is characterized by mass movements. "I am an enemy of the personal expression," the author said, "which is nothing but swindle and lyricism. In the epic, individuals and their so-called fates are of no use. Here they become the voice of the masses who are the real, natural, as well as epic, person."[30] Underlying this attitude are Döblin's philosophy of nature and his related poetics of the novel, but there is also his attempt to outdo Marinetti's *Marfarka le futuriste* to consider. It still remains to be seen whether Döblin's radical statements are softened by the novel itself. It goes without saying that there is no psychology here and no dramatic plot. Stylistic devices, such as the mere juxtaposition of nouns and verbs—without forming complete sentences— which stem from Futurism and whose basic effect is supposed to be dynamics and speed, take on a new meaning for Döblin. For he tries again and again to conjure up the soul of the living in its development in innumerable individual phenomena.

As always with Döblin, it is extraordinarily difficult to work out a plot summary in the face of the multitude of events and the onslaught of happenings. But, this time, Döblin has furnished some help in the "Bemerkungen zu *Berge Meere und Giganten*."

The first and second books show the hubristic, immeasurable development of technology to the point of its final breakdown. A technological master class is formed in which more and more women enroll. The masses are kept occupied by busy work and by the establishment of more and more new industries; but occasionally revolts occur. As with so many things in Döblin, technology wears a Janus head: as a manifestation of the human spirit it is admired; but by pushing man beyond nature, it threatens to destroy the bonds of nature and to lead to a total alienation from it. Thus in the novel there is no lack of individuals and groups who, on the basis of an antitechnological attitude, fight the dominance of machines and bureaucracies and desire to reincorporate man into natural environments. Thus, early in the novel, the calm and equanimity of nature is contrasted with human unrest and activity—and, once again, Döblin's skepticism toward action is evident:

They often stood gloomily in front of forests; and observed the sun-drenched tops of trees from a balcony; the deep-green pine trees which stretched their yellow-brown cones into the huge, silent heights, grew quietly upward: and man gnaws at himself, moves, gnaws. (BMG, 44)

The concentration of terrible weapons in the hands of the few creates mistrust and fear. Blows of desperation are levelled at machines; men like Targuniasch sacrifice themselves by plunging into the machines. Since the "vegetating masses" continuously streaming into the cities pose a latent threat, it is decided to keep the population occupied with war: the "uralic war" of the megalopolises London-New York against the Eastern half of the earth. This war releases enormous technological forces and leads to the destruction of large masses of people and of whole provinces in the East.

The third and fourth books, in which Marduk is the central figure, lead "to the goal of the whole work. All of mankind takes a long, enormously circuitous route in arriving at the same goal much later."[31] Marduk, Elina, and Jonathan blaze the trail which all mankind later follows.

Marduk continues the work of his predecessor, Marke, who had already driven the masses out of the cities and into the wilderness and had destroyed the machines. His efforts are supported by the "machinoclasts" (*"Maschinenstürmer"*) and the "deceivers" (*"Täuscher"*). Marduk begins his career as a brutal, power-mad technocrat. One of the most terrifying scenes in the novel is the destruction of his opponents. He has them destroyed by the overgrowth in a forest of the densest vegetation. He pursues his goals with extreme brutality: stemming technological progress, destroying superfluous machines, and dispersing the settlers. But he has to pay for this life with loneliness and self-loathing. A short love-hate relationship ties him to Marion Divoise, the "Balladeuse"—still another instance of the battle of the sexes. Since this relationship does not lead to a real union and thus to an overstepping of the individual's limits, and since it cannot free them from their terrible isolation, they can only tear each other to pieces. For the pride of the individual in them will not yield. The idyllic love between Marduk's friend Jonathan and Elina stands in contrast to this cramped relationship. After Jonathan's suicide, Marduk falls under the spell of Elina, and again—as nearly always in Döblin's works—the transformation occurs under the influence of genuine love:

Marduk and Elina were the first to lay down the weapons against nature and against themselves. Marduk was broken, melted by Elina and came back down to earth. He found himself behind and below his violent life.[32]

Through this love, the contact with the forces of nature is reestablished, and the conquest of one's own individuality and isolation become possible.

Books five to nine of the novel take up, in a larger context, the movement and transformation of Marduk. The fifth book depicts the "decline of the cities" (BMG, 263), for whose preservation battles are fought, since they are threatened by the bestialized masses. Fear and resignation are the basic feelings of this age. In order to regenerate the masses, new projects are planned which lead to new technological rape of the earth, however. The plan is to raise Greenland "from the ice, from the dripping ocean, from the heavy night" (BMG, 301). White Baker, who has joined the "Snakes" after having long been a member of the powerful London Senate, tries to deter Delvil (sounds like devil), the conceiver of the plan, from its execution:

She wrung her hands: "Say no. By heaven, by earth, Delvil say no. It's terrible. Let the earth rest. Look what you—I, too,—have already done to man. How they look, how they are destroyed. How you are destroyed. What you did in the war in Russia." (BMG, 332)

But her pleading is in vain. In Iceland, they discover the volcanic energy for thawing Greenland. "Man will find new powers. New human capabilities will be released, will rise incredibly above the earth and flex their muscles" (BMG, 341). This work is carried out with brutal consistency. People are mere material and are sacrificed by the thousands whenever necessary. A volcano is more important than a man.

With the help of energy gathered in "tourmaline veils" (*"Turmalinschleier"*), the ice of Greenland is to be melted. Again enormous energy is unleashed, but enormous numbers of people are sacrificed at the same time. But the motto is: "Think what you have already accomplished and overcome, and what lies behind you. We shall not give in. No one will give in. We will not be defeated. You will not forget who you are" (BMG, 400).

But even now there are individual dissonances in the gigantic symphony. As previously in the relationship between Jonathan and Elina, Marduk and Elina, in the "Snakes," in the games of the Fulbe, and in White Baker, the protest against the hubristic rape of the earth by technology and technocrats is voiced. This is done again by means of the relationship between the engineer, Holyhead, and the Syrian woman, Djedaida. And again love leads them to a genuine, deep, and true relationship to other people, to nature, and to themselves. But these idyllic episodes are drowned out by the orchestral noise of the great mass movements which continue to dominate the action.

The thawing of Greenland's ice generates monsters of life, "miscreants of an uncontrolled power" (BMG, 463) which threaten man by their enormous proliferation. As in the "Zauberlehrling," they are terrified by the powers which they have conjured up and which threaten to destroy them. For this reason, "an indefinite, dark feeling of guilt" (BMG, 470) begins to spread. But the rage and love for power on the part of the organizers (Delvil, for example) is only increased by this development:

He hated this world, the earth had done this to him, that fantastic, stupid, frightless power which arrayed itself in front of him and threw him down like a wild bull. . . . The earth's revenge was behind it all, but it would not do her much good. (BMG, 476)

Like many other individuals, Delvil has been torn out of the natural context of life and is only "after revenge and destruction" (BMG, 477). Thus he becomes the most extreme embodiment of inhumanity.

With the aid of the rediscovered "tourmaline veil," where "the soul of the living dwells" (BMG, 476), gigantic towers are erected along the coast as a protection against the monsters. People who are also implanted in them as building material swell up with the aid of the energy stored in the veil. At Delvil's command, the Scandinavian who rediscovered the lost veil is sunk into one of the towers. But, trusting in the powers of nature, he sings, dying, "his song of praise to the earth" (BMG, 481):

When I see your tower, Delvil, I praise the power of the earth. You will not conquer it. I praise the great power. I feel myself to be part of it. There is no boundary between it and me. I am not afraid. You will dissolve me. All right. I want to go there. (BMG, 481)

He commits himself to the anonymous primeval forces with which he is reunited in death. Thus he takes the path which many others have taken, and which the remnants of the Greenland settlers will also take in the end.

The ruling senates in the cities become more and more brutal and destroy the settlers. The cities become more and more subterranean, collapsing on the surface, while the remainder of the Greenland settlers gather around Kylin and experience a characteristic change which is by no means unexpected in this novel. In contrast to the giants, they acknowledge their own weakness and smallness and submit to the powers of nature which the others, in arrogant self-delusion, sought to control and join together in the adoration of fire. After the terrible experiences they have undergone, they now understand that the world is not merely material which they can ruthlessly exploit for their own purposes, but rather a living being. The volcano from which the flame shoots becomes the symbol of their insight.

Döblin believed that, wherever women surface, love, idylls, confidences, and psychological phenomena appear; thus, according to his notions, they had no place in an "epic work." It is all the more noteworthy that in this "novel" female characters appear for the first time as independently acting figures. Döblin himself, of course, immediately pointed out that they are not really independent, but are bound to the natural and to the epic landscape.[33] This change in his attitude toward women has been attributed to his acquaintance with Yolla Niclas, whom he met in 1921.[34]

At the center of the last book of the novel stands a woman,

Venaska. The "Snakes" mix in with Kylin's masses; one of their leaders is Venaska, whose whole power depends on the awe and love of the others. She gives herself up freely to the powers working in her, even to those of sexuality; and in her natural existence she makes the fig her goddess. Kylin sends her to the increasingly misanthropic and brutal giants, whose destructive rage threatens mankind anew. But Venaska perceives in them, too, "her blood, her brothers" (BMG, 576), and since she is herself nature and surrenders herself to the powers of nature, she is able to save the giants by returning them to anonymity. The closer she gets to the giants, the more intensely she fuses with the landscape. She sinks even deeper into nature in order eventually to sink into Delvil and thereby bring him back to nature. He returns—as do nearly all of Döblin's heroes—to the anonymity of the primeval powers:

"Dead brother, now everything is all right. Now I have you. Stretch out. You have legs, sink down. Down. Down. We are sinking. Also, it is good to sink." It was no longer Delvil, extended into mountains, sea, forest, flowing apart. It was no longer Delvil. (BMG, 579)

In the face of the enormous suffering which the hubris of man has brought upon the earth, and in the face of the decaying cities, Kylin wants to find the cleansing and purifying power of pain—another recurrent theme in Döblin's works.

The travellers to Iceland establish a new order in the country; they are viewed as the victors over the giants, and they are imitated in their veneration of fire. Everywhere people return to nature:

People empathized anew with the storm, the rain, the earth, the movements of the sun and stars. People approached the gentle plants, the animals. . . . But people already prayed joyfully, breathing slowly, to the flickering light, to the great powers which had saved everybody and now had rekindled their spirits. . . . Hourly, people were surrounded by mysterious powers; . . . (BMG, 583)

This sounds like a general condemnation of technology and like a return to the idyll. But on the last pages of the book, in the last conversations it becomes evident that this is not a retreat from the problem but the yielding of an untenable position. The technological achievements of man are not to be cast aside, but only their misuse by a race that overestimates its own possibilities and despises man and the eternal laws of nature. It is in this sense that Kylin and Ten Keir erect a memorial placard to the giants, for "they were powerful people" (BMG, 587). Only when they raped nature did they call forth those destructive powers. This return to nature becomes significant only through the experience of the past, because it occurs at the height of man's perfection of power, after the uralic war and after the thawing of Greenland have been endured. In this sense, the survivors of these catastrophes are the true giants. They have "power, real knowledge, and humility" (BMG, 588).

Thus, at the end, the book returns humbly to the eternal power of nature, to the attitude of the "Dedication": to the consciousness of being carried by an unending nature worthy of religious veneration. "'Sacrifice' and 'humility' had been found, the perception, but not the inner power," wrote Döblin in the "Epilog."[35]

Döblin must have been aware that he demanded too much from his readers. He reworked the novel and republished it in 1932 under the title *Giganten. Ein Abenteuerbuch* ("Giants. An Adventure Book"). The "Dedication" was eliminated. As in *Berlin Alexanderplatz,* a thematic outline introduces the story, and the various paragraphs of the outline serve as epigraphs for the chapters of the novel. The development and meaning of the machine are now more expressly emphasized and form a better scaffolding for the plot. Out of nine books Döblin makes eight, which, in part, receive new names.

Döblin remarked that in 1932 he was not the same person as in 1924 and that he was not able merely to shorten and cross out but wanted something quite different; thus he calls *Giganten* a new book. However, it can easily be shown that he merely effected a change of accent. While, at the end of *Berge Meere und Giganten,* the people observe nature and empathize with it, grasp its mystery and its immovability in all events, Döblin now sides more with the active people: "The new book has a man behind it who recognizes a human task, who knows its sense and sees it even in nature, who knows the role of will, power, and perception and accepts encroachments on nature into the bargain."[36] More than before, Döblin now celebrates man's autonomy and pride of creation: "We have a proud, free, self-

History and Science Fiction

responsible ego in us."[37] To be sure, this consciousness leads to a "gigantic degeneration."[38] A look at the last section of *Giganten* supplements and corrects Döblin's self-interpretation. He consciously seeks an equalization between the eternal laws of nature and the technological efforts of man, the latter being judged negatively at the end of *Berge Meere und Giganten*. The concept of "law" is used as a formula of this equalization: "No decision was made in favor of machines, but also none in favor of the settlers. There was a third concept: the law!" (G, 370). Again—and thus basically the experience of the earlier work is strengthened—the laws of nature provide the boundary which human activity seeks to break. Upon this period of activity, leading to degeneration, there follows a time of peace, of the quieting of the machine soul:

The great pendulum has swung back again. Upon the long flowing exhalation there followed a deep fulfilling inhalation. They had created the machine, had freed it, let themselves be led by it; they had gathered the powers of nature and subjected them; they were the masters of the earth,—now—enough had been done. Enough had been done. There is a time for acting. There is a time for not acting. It was necessary to watch and to wander, but also to stand and to lie. (G, 370)

CHAPTER 6

Mythology and Modern Existence

I Manas. Epische Dichtung

A greater difference than that between *Berge Meere und Giganten* and *Manas*—both thematically and stylistically—is hardly imaginable. After the depiction of the visionary future of a modern industrial world and its end, Döblin turned to India, more precisely, to a mythical world.

In the "Epilog," Döblin asserted that with *Berge Meere und Giganten* he had finished with the masses:

> With it I had finished the way of the masses and great collective powers. Indeed, up to then, up to the book of the "Giants" I was fascinated by the created world and had taken its part. With the exhausting effort of the book of the "Giants" I had done enough.[1]

As so much in Döblin, this sketch, written in the retrospective view of a convert, cannot be taken too literally. The caesura which Döblin would like to make here is by no means as abrupt as he believes. For although mass movements are more conspicuous in the early novels, the individual, his problems, and his decisions are by no means forgotten. In *Berge Meere und Giganten* it is the single voices which are contrasted with the chorus of the masses—and which finally come to dominate. Even if there is no basic reorientation, an important transformation does take place.

In the preparatory studies for *Wang-lun*, there are already references to Shiva and Mount Kailas, and the "Dedication" to *Berge Meere und Giganten* was probably suggested by an Indian hymn. The first impulse seems to have been a most concrete one: the fascination by an exotic world to which Döblin, thanks to his unbounded imagination, could easily transport himself:

> I once found (in Berlin, in the municipal library am Marstall) a

Mythology and Modern Existence

travelogue from India full of pictures and a lot of history. The milieu was strange to me and adventurous, tropically rich. I was fascinated by the reports on Hinduism, on Shiva, the god, and on a Realm of the Dead.[2]

No less important than this factual curiosity was Döblin's interest in Buddhism in the early twenties. There can be no doubt that Döblin was a deeply religious man. His study of Taoism, Buddhism, his own philosophy of nature, his attacks on Christianity and, finally, his conversion bear ample witness to this. All of these religions were stations in his search for a binding metaphysical or religious creed. In an essay which appeared in 1919 under the provocative title "Jenseits von Gott"[3] Döblin, in his own peculiar rigor, declared Christianity defunct but simultaneously demanded a new mythology which, for a long time, he found in his own philosophy of nature.

The transition from Taoism to Buddhism in Döblin's thinking is important, for the latter allows for greater human initiative. As Döblin expressed it:

The Tao proclaims: Action changes nothing.
Buddha, however—.
This difference between the silent, speechless aspect of Tao's teachings and Buddha's—for all his delicacy—decisive, Promethean lifting out of oneself.[4]

But Döblin criticizes Buddha's teachings, which attest to a greater inclination toward human individual decisions, from the point of view of his philosophy. Buddha was overcome by pain, age, and death, and preached extinction, the urge to be released from the bond of existence and desires. But Döblin insists that age and death, like everything else, belong to life. For him, nothing is dead; for dead matter, is only a different form of life. The result is that our individual form is ephemeral, temporary, and that we should never lose ourselves completely in it. Thus man is not only moved—as Buddha believes—by his desires, which he must extinguish, but he is a descendent of the great primeval forces to which he must, and wants to, return:

The source of my powers and my life is no mystic god whom I would like to pray to with the so-called pious people. The source of my powers and my life is also no eternal mass of desires which cause pain that I must flee with Buddha. Alkalis, acids, hydrogen, oxygen, carbon dioxide, liquids, solids, electric currents, that is what I am. I incline to their soul, from them I come, that is my lineage. This is my patriotism.[5]

This is unmistakably the thought complex underlying *Berge Meere und Giganten*. *Manas*, on the other hand, mirrors the altercation between the philosophy of nature and Buddhism which offers a new challenge to Döblin's thought.

Another experience also intrudes here: that of Döblin's trip to Poland, undertaken in 1924. The observations he made on this journey corroborated some of his fundamental beliefs. Thus he noted on the occasion of the Feast of the Tabernacles in Warsaw's Jewish quarter:

I cannot help myself: as I walk through the vestibules and see tabernacle after tabernacle, I am filled with astonishment, with awe, and with joy: the spirit lives, the spirit is active in nature. The spirit will hold them together. No so-called misfortune made rubble of them because they did not want it to. As they wander through the millenia, falter, and are driven, they are a symbol of the only thing that has a future, birth, creation: of the spirit and power of the ego. (RiP, 98)

As always, the idea of a supra-ego, of an intellectual power which radiates into man and nature is at the center of Döblin's thought. Repeatedly he sees in nature the power of this ego: But of equal importance with nature is the human spirit and will:

Immeasurable nature, this thing here that I see seems strongest to me. It does so over and over again. I do not need to correct myself. A piece of it lies in front of me: the sea, the liquid garden full of animals and plants, which the wind dominates. And the second, the second strongest? The—soul. The spirit, the will of man. I have seen courageous herds of people. Oppressed herds of people. That people may not succumb in worship is crystal clear. That people may change, renew, tear down, be obliged to tear down is clear to me. The spirit and the will are legitimate, fertile, and strong.
There is a god-willed independence in the individual man, in each individual. . . . All by himself everyone carries his head between his shoulders. (RiP, 344)

The second experience which moved Döblin deeply occurred

Mythology and Modern Existence

in the Church of St. Mary in Cracow. Mary, floating on a quarter moon, represented for him the unity of soul, God, and nature. Of greater importance, however, was the figure of Christ, the "man of suffering," the "just man," the "hanged man." Christ becomes the symbol of sacrifice, of pain, and of misery, and thus of a basic experience of human existence. But it is a pain which opens one's eyes—an idea that also reappears in *Manas*. So terrible is the experience and the message of Christ that it must be framed in beauty to be bearable. It is this secularized form of Christ which repeatedly appeared in the novels thereafter and prepared the way for the author's conversion. But that is only the one side; for human greatness, independence, and creativity, symbolized by the machine, is juxtaposed with the experience of the necessity for sacrifice and pain. In fact, Döblin's image of man is dominated by this polarity:

I praised Cracow, the Church of St. Mary, the Crucified One, the Just One. They live. The most ancient thing is always the newest. But these machines here are also genuine, strong, living steel. They have my heart. I don't care how they are connected with the Crucified One and the Just One.
I—and even if the contradiction leads to nonsense and to tell—I praise them both. (RiP, 326)

The epic poem *Manas* must be studied against the background of the dispute between Döblin's philosophy of nature and Buddhism on the one hand and the ambivalence of his experiences during the journey to Poland on the other.

Manas is one of Döblin's best but least known works. For this writer, style was something that had to come from the material and the basic ideas. Thus he was only consistent when he chose the epic form for the shaping of a mythological subject. The linguistic experiments of the *Sturm* circle and of Futurism stood him in good stead and helped him to shape the language of his epic. There are passages in his previous and subsequent novels which are close to rhythmically shaped free verse; indeed, rhyme is occasionally used.[6] Döblin, who hated lyricism all his life, created a very original form of free verse which works especially well with associations of sounds, variations, and rhythmic repetitions. Although the theme was a challenge for his inclination toward formal experiments and for his unbound fantasy, *Manas*—

because of its clear structure and strict organization—is the most "classic" of his works.

The following, in the words of the author, is the course of the action:

I got stuck on the reports of Hinduism, of Shiva, the god, and of a Realm of the Dead. I saw a man entering, one from our world who wants to be torn apart by the misery he finds in this world of the dead. He wants all earthly pains to fall upon him, he wants to unite himself with all suffering because he knows (from a war), that we are all one and the same, brothers, the murderers and the murdered, the executioner and his victim.
He risks the journey of terror and collapses. But Sawitri, his wife (she is a goddess, divine love), lifts him up; he returns as a new man, as a half-god.[7]

Again it is pain which throws man out of his accustomed bounds and makes his previous life seem questionable. And, to be sure, suffering befalls Manas at the moment of his greatest triumph, i.e., upon his victorious return from battle. According to Döblin's conviction, suffering opens men's eyes, and thus Manas "saw the horror of the creature in battle" (Ma, 11). What is more: in an enemy he recognized his brother—as Wang-lun did in the robber. The doctrine of the identity of all beings must have particularly attracted Döblin to Hinduism—apart from its being an essential element of the Expressionist cosmology. The important moment at which the transformation takes place in Manas, when he stands at the window receiving the ovations of the crowd and is suddenly struck by pain and by the insight into suffering, constantly returns, like a leitmotif, to his consciousness—just as the murder of the captain is always in Wang-lun's mind. When his teacher, Puto, points out to him that pain is immanent in the world, Manas wants to experience it even more strongly and tries to seek it out in the Realm of the Dead. In his desire for pain, Manas oversteps the boundary of the Realm of the Dead and begins to absorb the errant souls of the dead. The suffering which he experiences vicariously forces him to his knees; he wants to surrender his ego, for "he can no longer tolerate existence" (Ma, 44). He wants to go to Shiva, the many-faced god, to surrender completely—that, too, a typical sign of his transformation, of the obliteration of his ego (*"Entichung"*). Puto

Mythology and Modern Existence

is to break the chain which connects them—and, symbolically, Manas's chains—with life at the same time.

A final intensification comes from the meeting with the soul of a man Manas has slain. Manas's pain is boundless. He perceives the evil in his life, which he attempts to extinguish, although it always lives on. He does not want to live any more: "I lay myself down" (Ma, 60). This last convulsion throws him into a deep unconsciousness which three demons, who hope in this way to escape from the Realm of the Dead, use to slip into him. In attempting to fight them, Puto kills Manas and returns with the corpse to Udaipur. Sawitri, Manas's wife, does not recognize her husband in the corpse; since she feels that he will return, she does not want to be cremated with him. In their love story, which is narrated at this point, their wordless attraction to each other is depicted. This feeling affects her now so strongly that she begins to search for Manas. Like Venaska on her journey to the giants, Sawitri blends completely with nature; she speaks to all beings; and the wild animals leave her alone. With the abandonment of her individuality, she becomes the lover of a bushman; and now—typically enough for Döblin—she hears Manas's voice. At the tree under which Puto erroneously killed Manas, she feels through nature what happened here because she is nature.

She, too, meets the souls of the dead in the Field of the Dead and takes part in their fate, often one of love in which her own unconditional devotion is mirrored. Sawitri is in nature; she accepts all things, affirms all things, for she is not only herself, but also everything else:

> In this body lived not only Sawitri,
> Sawitri and Manas, too,
> The shouting dark bushman
> The barren endless steppes, the mysterious tree,
> Magic sleep under the moon. (Ma, 156)

Because she herself is everything, she is also creative nature, and thus she can bear Manas again, can be at once mother and lover. Shiva, who takes her to him, bows before her all-conquering love; she is the "lover, delver into all worlds" (Ma, 231). The third and last book of *Manas* portrays the return to earth and to human society of a Manas raised to a mythical level.[8]

Previously, Döblin's figures had had to align themselves with, indeed subordinate themselves to, the laws of nature and to the context of life that extended beyond the single individual. They had to be prepared for sacrifice, humility, self-abandonment, for only thus, in connection with the great, anonymous primeval powers did their life acquire meaning, profundity, and truth. In Manas, Döblin for the first time conceived a figure who is the equal of these powers, indeed sometimes even superior to them. But this figure is no longer a man. He is a mythical half-god. Manas chains up the demons who had misused his body and subjugates them. Then he makes them carry him out to sea.

The role which water, as one of the great organic primeval powers, plays in the philosophical thought of Döblin must always be kept in mind if one is to understand this episode in its full significance. Kylin humbly reveres the power of fire with his forces, but Manas speaks and plays with the water that cradles him but does not swallow him up. Thus the conquest of the natural powers is symbolically shown.

All Döblin's figures are in search of themselves and their position in the world; for Manas this is equally true. This explains his return to the Thar desert, the site of his great victories, and to his father Jajarta. He explains to the latter that the living are already dead, for they are weak and would blow away like the souls on the Field of the Dead; their life is only a dream. To Puto's question of who they are, Manas responds:

> Look at the sky at night, tonight.
> There is the train of a robe.
> Then someone goes and pulls the train behind him.
> It whirls up dust, so much dust.
> The stars are this dust
> And the earth and the flowers and people
> And the gods and everything else. . . .
> I—feel the one who pulls the train, Puto.
> Although I whirl with the dust myself, I feel him. (Ma, 307 f.)

For the understanding of this last part of the epic the knowledge of Döblin's philosophy of nature is a necessary prerequisite. The awareness of the individual—here of Manas—of being carried and borne along by the ego, engenders the cosmic feeling which Manas articulates here; he feels the power which moves

Mythology and Modern Existence

everything, and this feeling gives his own existence meaning and greatness. But Manas is by no means the moving power. For to Puto's question if he is the one who pulls the train, Manas answers: "Lead me not into temptation,/Lead me not into temptation" (Ma, 308). An overestimation of his own powers would—as in *Berge Meere und Giganten*—lead to hubris and self-destruction. Manas has a presentiment of that.

Manas is a half-god who is happy about his preternatural power; but, on the other hand, there is the feeling of smallness, the awareness of being, even with this preternatural power, only a speck of dust in the endless and enormous cosmic motion. This polarity of feeling permeates the third book of the epic. In a masterful review of *Manas*, Robert Musil proclaimed this tension of feeling to be the greatest aspect of the work.[9] It is the tension between "manic presumption and deep depression" which constitutes the basic feeling of the work; the feeling of greatness, freedom, and independence on the one hand, and that of smallness, weakness, and transitoriness on the other. This awareness of one's own nothingness and weakness also results in the wish to dissolve one's own individual form and to return to the unconscious anonymity of the great primeval powers which, alone, are eternal and true. Thus Manas speaks to the Bo tree—for everything in this epic is animated and feels and speaks in a legendary, magic way:

> Dissolve my flesh from my hands,
> From my face.
> My flesh, tremble away with them, with everything,
> We tremble together.
> My flesh, blood, my feeling, do not rest!
> The air, the light, the smiling countenance,
> The treading feet, the floating boats:
> Press into me.
> Fall upon me.
> All.
> We flee together, flee, fly together. (Ma, 314 f.)

But, on the other hand, joy in one's own existence, the "I am, I live" (Ma, 318) is repeatedly encountered.

Manas confronts the greatest challenge with the feeling of

power and the joy in one's own existence in the city of Amber, where a priest preaches Buddhistic Nirvana to him:

> It is better to be extinguished, in order to make an end of it.
> There has to be an end, you understand, Manas?
> Perhaps you are enough of a man to understand that.
> We have to spit out this life sometime,
> Like rotten fruit, a mushroom which will poison us. (Ma, 335)

But Manas does not want to be extinguished; indeed this idea insults his feeling of his own power and greatness. In uncontrolled anger, he rages against Shiva's temple and destroys it. The god, in whom nature is embodied, enters the scene and demands Manas's submission. There is a fight between the two, but Manas gains the upper hand by invoking the ego, the intellectual power to whom they both owe their existence, that stands over nature, over Shiva, for even the latter is only "a creature, a descendent" (Ma, 359):

> Manas invoked the ego
> That makes lips lips, tongue tongue, hands hands.
> Manas, oh Manas, Sawitri's beloved child,
> Invoked the soul of souls, the secret, hidden ego,
> That is as hidden as the air to the eyes
> And carries everything as the air carries the birds. (Ma, 355 f.)

Manas, who is haunted by the unnerving experience in Amber, becomes involved in the worries of man—just as the penitent Shiva suspends himself in fire—in order not to forget; just as pain drove him into the Field of the Dead, so pain alone can preserve his experiences, the twofold experiences of greatness and smallness. To those who weep without hope:

> What remains of the man
> Who gives his soul to fire,
> His breath to the wind,
> His eyes to the sun,
> His blood to the water.

He calls:

> You! You!
> Do not sink!

Mythology and Modern Existence

> Do not give in!
> Shiva lives!
> You are not living yet. Not yet! You are not living yet! (Ma, 371)

When, at the end, it is stated: "He is not extinguished. Not extinguished./Manas is not extinguished" (Ma, 371), it is clear that Manas represents the eternal power in man which presses out beyond him and struggles, always gaining the upper hand despite all depressions. But to say it once again: Manas is a mythical demigod, not a man.

For Döblin, there was never a logical or rational measuring of positions, and his work, particularly *Manas*, is done an injustice if one looks for a rigidly closed intellectual system. Döblin is beholden to a secularized "godless mysticism," to use Fritz Mauthner's term. Thus the meaning of the book lies in the upward and downward movement of feeling depicted in a mythical action for which Döblin has found the proper language, so that the otherwise touchy attempt to revive the epic genre may be called successful.

II Berlin Alexanderplatz

With this masterpiece, Döblin, now fifty years old and at the zenith of his creativity,[10] returned from distant India and mythical times to the Berlin of the 1920's. Because his publisher did not know what to make of the title *Berlin Alexanderplatz* (*Alexanderplatz, Berlin*), Döblin had to add the subtitle *Die Geschichte vom Franz Biberkopf* (*The Story of Franz Biberkopf*). Although its action is limited chiefly to Eastern Berlin and its underworld figures, the book, which appeared in 1929, is the first and only major novel about a big city in German literature. In his bibliography, Wolfgang Peitz lists ten different editions, some of which had a very large circulation.[11] The book was translated into eight languages, including all the major tongues.[12] The novel—or rather, in Döblin's terminology, the "epic work"—is centered on the Alexanderplatz in the proletarian section of Eastern Berlin, an area that Döblin knew like the palm of his hand, since he grew up and worked there. The central figure of the novel is the Berlin transportation worker Franz Biberkopf, and all events and episodes are related to him, even if the connection is not always immediately clear.

Biberkopf's story begins with his release from prison where he has served his time for the manslaughter of his girl friend, Ida. Three times he attempts to "conquer" Berlin; but three times something that looks like fate strikes him. Theodore Ziolkowski has pointed out that, each time, this development echoes the triad of Greek tragedy: hamartia, peripeteia, and catastrophe.[13] Release brings the shock of freedom. In prison everything was regulated, but now Biberkopf must run his own life again. The skidding roofs, which he believes he sees, betray his insecurity. His panic chases him into back courts, where he tries to find his courage by singing patriotic songs. Some Jews have pity on him and tell him stories. When Franz tries to regain his self-confidence in the affirmation of his virility, he fails miserably. Only when he returns to Minna, the sister of the girl he killed, and seduces her, does he regain control of himself. He promises to himself and the world that he will keep clean. But keeping clean in the world in which he lives is an extremely difficult matter: "Stay respectable and keep to yourself. That's my idea" (AB, 73).

Soon Franz has a girl friend again, his Polish Lina, and to earn money he peddles tie clasps on Rosenthal Square (Rosenthaler Platz). Later on he sells Nazi newspapers: "Franz now peddles racist, pro-Nordic papers. He is not against the Jews, but he is for law and order. For law and order must reign in Paradise, as everyone should recognize" (AB, 97). His connection with the propaganda organ of the Nazis causes resentment in many of his socialist friends and acquaintances and leads to vehement discussions in the bars around the Alexanderplatz—which mirror the incipient economic and political crisis, a period in which the weakness of the Weimar Republic becomes increasingly evident.

But then the first "blow" is struck against Franz. As a door-to-door shoelace salesman, he was very successful with a widow. She had coffee with him, gave him money, "and then a little bit more" (AB, 134). Franz boasts of his success to his companion, Lüders who blackmails the widow, and when Franz returns to her, he is not even admitted. When he has learned the real reason, he is disappointed and hurt that his plan to try to keep clean has been ruined by the world. Deeply hurt, he withdraws into isolation and begins to drink.

Yet this first "blow," the first warning of fate, was relatively

Mythology and Modern Existence

gentle. Franz quickly recovers. "But it wasn't so bad after all, Franz Biberkopf is being spared for a harder fall" (AB, 153). He is quickly on top of things again and returns to the Jews, the witnesses of his anxiety about freedom after his release, to play them a farewell march, as if to reassert himself by doing it. In his unconscious attempt to make connection with his earlier life, to establish a certain continuity, he returns once more to Minna, but her husband slams the door in his face. From his window he witnesses a burglary—an anticipation of his later fate and a warning, for he himself is later drawn into a crime.

Reinhold, who becomes Franz's real antagonist, is a member of the Pums gang specializing in burglaries, a fact that Franz is unaware of at the moment. At first, Biberkopf carries on "a spirited white slavery" with him, for Reinhold is in the habit of changing girl friends as he changes shirts. Biberkopf takes them off his hands as soon as Reinhold gets an appetite for a new girl, and passes them on as soon as Reinhold sends him the next discarded number. Soon Biberkopf grows tired of this strange trade and decides to "educate" Reinhold by persuading his latest girl friend to stick it out and also by warning the new one. This is a fateful decision for Franz! He boasts—in Reinhold's presence—to a friend about his pedagogic success and thereby calls Reinhold's attention to it.

Finally he becomes involved in a burglary. Members of the Pums gang, including Reinhold, have persuaded him to pick up "fruit" with them. Unsuspectingly, Biberkopf goes along and realizes too late what is really happening. When a car pursues them on their return trip, Reinhold seizes the opportunity to take his revenge on Biberkopf. He shoves him out of the moving car, so that Biberkopf is run over by the pursuing car. A second, heavier blow has been struck against him.

But Biberkopf is, once more, saved. His old friends, the pimp, Herbert Wischow, and his girl friend, Eva, take him to a clinic in Magdeburg, where his right arm is amputated at the shoulder. Biberkopf keeps silent about the background of the "traffic accident." His will to live is unbroken; he wants to battle against the thing that threatens him so maliciously. Soon he has a girl again, his Mieze, whom he really loves; and he becomes a fence and a pimp. He resumes his connection with the Pums gang, which accepts him as a member after some hesitation.

[101]

Reinhold has a magnetic attraction for him, and thus the battle between the two is resumed. Again it is Franz's pride that brings about his misfortune: he brags about Mieze's love and faithfulness. In a scene reminiscent of Hebbel's *Gyges und sein Ring*, he tries to display the love and faithfulness of his girl to Reinhold, who is hidden in a bed.[14] But just at that moment Mieze—sensing nothing—confesses to him that she is in love with the nephew of her "patron." Beside himself with rage, Franz nearly kills her—just as he killed Ida. He has learned nothing. But even before that, when Biberkopf mentioned her, Reinhold had silently decided to take her away from him.

Mieze, who loves Franz in spite of everything, tries to get to the bottom of the mystery in his relationship with the Pums gang and Reinhold. But, like Franz, she overestimates her powers. She flirts with Reinhold but, when on a walk in a woods she resists his advances, he murders her. The third blow has been struck against Franz.

After a falling out in the Pums gang, Reinhold's accomplice informs the police, and Franz and Reinhold are sought under a warrant of arrest. Herbert and Biberkopf, disguised with an artificial arm and a wig, look for the murderer without finding him. When one of the disreputable bars which Franz frequents is raided, Franz resists with a pistol and is arrested. He is identified, and since he is obviously not in full possession of his mental powers, he is admitted to the asylum Berlin-Buch.

Reinhold lets himself be captured after a petty burglary, in order to get into prison, where he feels safest. In a weak moment, he relates his story to a fellow convict, and the latter betrays him. Reinhold is brought to trial and found guilty. Biberkopf appears at the trial but does not testify against him.

In the meantime, Franz had lain in Buch in a stupor. Because he refused all food, he had to be fed intravenously. He wanted to give up, die, and return, body and soul, to nature. Death spoke with him. But Biberkopf—as the author never tires of telling us—is an uncommon common man. He rises again and gets a chance at making a new beginning. He becomes a porter's helper in a local factory.

A novel is more than its plot. That is especially true of *Berlin Alexanderplatz*, which is not only the story of Franz Biberkopf but also the depiction of a totality, of Eastern Berlin around the

Mythology and Modern Existence

Alexanderplatz, where Franz and the others move about. This totality—a favorite expression of literary Expressionism—is achieved by means of the montage or collage,[15] as it is found, for example, in the pictures of the Cubists and especially, in Kurt Schwitters' MERZ pictures: self-sufficient elements of reality are mounted into the novel and are given a new function and a changed reality in the context of the novel without giving up their true identity. Thus all sorts of "literary" productions which a person of our century encounters daily find their way into the novel: hit songs, advertising blurbs, news reports, weather reports, political slogans, theater programs, statistics, etc. Döblin cut such texts out and pasted them into his manuscript.[16] In a manner previously unknown, the novel thus presents the world directly by going beyond merely describing it. Often these texts stand in apparent isolation as foreign bodies, and occasionally they appear in the stream of consciousness of the figures or of the narrator. Because the world in its immediate fullness forces its way into the figures from outside, because its governing consciousness is inundated by the automatism of the stream of consciousness fed internally or externally, the personality of the figures dissolves, and the dividing line between subject and object is obliterated. Here again Döblin's philosophical insight becomes visible. There is no isolated thing, no isolated individual. Everything is linked in a "real nexus" ("*Realzusammenhang*")[17] with the surrounding world. Thus even in the style the theme of the novel becomes evident: the guilt of isolation and the overestimation of his own power on the part of the isolated individual.

Most of what is mounted into the novel helps to create not only the atmosphere of the work, but has a direct bearing on Biberkopf's fate and on the overall theme. The creative imagination of the reader is indispensable; it has often to uncover the hidden connections and thus to create the work anew; in a way, the reader recreates the narrative process. The texts, partly unaltered, partly freely revised by the author for his own purposes, are frequently used with ironic intent. The epigraph to the chapter in which Franz discovers his temporary impotence is a stock market report and states laconically: "Market dull, later bears very active, Hamburg depressed, London weaker" (AB, 28). The possible reasons for Franz's sexual failure are alluded to in the form of a pharmaceutical description of the sexual therapeutic,

Testifortan. The victory of Franz's girl friend, the Polish Lina, over the newspaper boy is accentuated by quotations from Kleist's *Prinz Friedrich von Homburg*. When Franz has recovered from the deceit practiced on him by the little Lüders, the chapter epigraph quotes a child's song: "Gallop-a-trot, gallop-a-trot, little horsey starts trotting again" (AB, 205). Other texts appear as swimming freely in the consciousness of Franz and other figures. Senseless verses roll through his mind when he stops with the first prostitute; later they reappear quite unexpectedly. No limits are set to the free association of the narrator or Franz, and it is not always clear who is really speaking, reading, or thinking. The narrator is a devil of a fellow. He presents the events with an obviously didactic intent and speaks through the mask of a minstrel (*Bänkelsänger*), as becomes particularly evident in the Prologue.[18] He speaks a coarse, popular language and often uses primitive rhymes. One sees him, as it were, pointing to his chalk board: "To listen to this and to meditate on it will be of benefit to many who, like Franz Biberkopf, live in a human skin, and, like Franz Biberkopf, ask more of life than a piece of bread and butter" (AB, 2). In short, Döblin draws on the same subliterary traditions as his friend Bertolt Brecht.

The narrator, interpolating things into the novel, compares Franz ironically with Orestes. He explains Ida's murder with the help of Newton's laws. He is—when he pleases—omnipresent and omniscient and recites the whole biography of arbitrary random characters, including their obituaries. He describes his tour of the Berlin slaughterhouse—with abundant use of reports from the cattle market inserted—and loosely retells the Biblical stories of Job, Abraham, and Isaac. He admonishes his hero and explains things to the audience (the reader).

With this whole arsenal of technical devices—only the most important of which are mentioned here—Döblin created a work that comes closest to fulfilling his concept of the epic because it strives for the dynamic portrayal of a living situation, and no longer the description of an isolated biography. Although literature can only portray events in time, that is, in succession, Döblin does achieve the illusion of the simultaneity of different events—a technique he had seen in the pictures of the Futurists—the illusion of external and internal simultaneity, of a parallel in personal and political events. Döblin repeatedly stressed that this

Mythology and Modern Existence

method was derived from the visual arts, not from Joyce, whom Döblin was reproached with imitating:

> Well, even if I do imitate and need a model, why must I go to James Joyce, the Irishman, when I have learned the style, the method which he uses (fabulous, I admire it) at the same place where he learned it, from the Expressionists, Dadaists, and so forth.[19]

The reader, confused by the constantly changing narrative perspective and by the multitude of impressions crowding in on him, receives a true image of the chaotic, disconnected, eternally changing —life of the modern city. But under closer scrutiny it is evident that almost all the carefully arranged episodes relate to Biberkopf; everything is talking to him, but he cannot hear. Life, which is "a radical cure" (AB, 2) for him becomes meaningful at the end. Like all of Döblin's heroes, Biberkopf goes through "a process of revelation of a special kind" (AB, 632) in the course of which his eyes are opened. After his release from prison, he appears with the idea of keeping clean and of withstanding the world on his own. Proud as he is, he relies on his own strength, on his own autonomous individuality. But life breaks him of his rigid, surly attitude; he wants to assert his self, but he must learn to abandon himself, to be a victim:

> Sacrifice was the theme of *Berlin Alexanderplatz*. The pictures of the slaughterhouse, of the sacrifice of Isaac, the ubiquitous quotation: "There is a Reaper, Death yclept" should have made one aware of it. "Good" Franz Biberkopf with his claim on life cannot be broken until his death. But he has to be broken, he must surrender himself, not merely externally.[20]

Eventually, all events reveal a hidden connection with Franz's fate. Even the stories which the Jews tell him to calm him down are parables demonstrating positive and negative behavior to him. Without Franz's being able to recognize their meaning, they show the need for assimilation and submission on the one hand and the dangers of overestimation of one's self on the other. "Franz has had his own experiences. Franz knows life. Franz knows who he is" (AB, 47). Early in the novel, the "voice," later unmasked as the voice of Death, addresses a warning and an urgent admonition to him. The first blow, Lüder's deception, is brought on by Franz's own arrogance and blindness, but has only a temporary effect. In a scene of symbolic purgation, he undoes the act; he returns to the Jews to blow "a farewell march to the Jews" (AB, 164): a final rejection of their instruction, whose meaning for his own fate has escaped him. "The eleventh commandment says: Don't let 'em bluff you" (AB, 168). Franz is not shaken from his self-assured, boastful attitude.

The stuttering Reinhold finally becomes Franz's fate. Reinhold has a strange attraction for Franz, similar to that which Wallenstein exerted on Ferdinand. Critics have rightly pointed to the erotic root of such bondage to power. He is "that cold force which nothing in life can change" (AB, 576). Before his meeting with Reinhold, Death again speaks urgently and warningly to Franz; it tries to convince Biberkopf of its strength and power but is laughed to scorn by him who believes only in his own power. In his own eyes, Franz is unshakable.

From this point on, Death speaks more and more strongly in the novel. Before his encounter with Reinhold, the Berlin slaughterhouse is described with great emphasis on the death of the animals. Later, much like a leitmotif, fragments of this description recur continuously. The titles of the sections make it unmistakably clear that this is not merely a random description of a locale, but that the episode has a bearing on Biberkopf's fate. The titles are quotations from the third chapter of Ecclesiastes: "For it happens alike with Man and Beast, as the Beast dies, so Man dies, too" (AB, 172). And: "And they all have the same Breath, and Men have no more than Beasts" (AB, 188). The unity of all created beings is stressed; everything is created and must succumb to death. A little later, the folk song of the Reaper Death appears for the first time: "There is a Reaper Death yclept. Hath power which the Lord hath kept. When he 'gins his scythe to whet, keener it grows and keener yet, soon will he slash, man must endure the gash" (AB, 246).

During the tour of the slaughterhouse, undertaken by the narrator, the dialogue between Job and the voice is inserted. In order to be made applicable to Biberkopf's life—Job becomes Franz's mirror image—the Old Testament tale is modified: Job does not want to be cured, for recovery would presuppose his self-abandonment, the admission of his impotence and ignorance. He would like to be able to resist—not by chance does the key

Mythology and Modern Existence

word of *Wang-lun* resurface here. Franz, too, can only be cured of his blindness when he is ready to surrender himself.

But the self-assured and arrogant Franz does not recognize the menace posed by Reinhold. He feels compelled to educate him and boasts of his pedagogic successes to him and to his friend Meck: "What do you say, Meck, we'll create law and order in this world, we'll smash this thing, let 'em come, if they want anything out of us" (AB, 262). But even the second blow, struck by Reinhold who, during the burglary, is revealed as a cold-blooded and unscrupulous criminal, is not sufficient. On the contrary, Franz now wants to test his strength on Reinhold: "I have something to do, something will happen, I won't stir from here, I am Franz Biberkopf" (AB, 302).

Before Franz makes the fateful trip back to Reinhold, another free rendition of a story from the Old Testament is inserted in modified form: that of Abraham's sacrifice. The stress now lies on Isaac's acceptance of his own sacrifice. The sacrifice must be carried out with his full awareness, or else it cannot be offered. Only in the conscious insight into the necessity of self-abandonment does the sacrifice have meaning—and become superfluous. For it all depends first and foremost on the readiness, not on the execution. Franz is not ready for, and capable of, this choice. He seeks self-assertion, not self-abandonment. He does not want to be overthrown: "Just sit tight, hold on firm, that's Reinhold, that's the way he noses around, only watch out he don't knock you down" (AB, 405). The duel with Reinhold intensifies and reaches its climax in the murder of Mieze. Like Franz, she, too, overestimates her powers in this battle and has to die as a result. A verse from the third chapter of Ecclesiastes is interwoven into this chapter: "To everything there is a season, to everything, to everything" (AB, 481). Thus the mortality of man is stressed anew.

In spite of the repeated advice of the voice, only at the very end when Franz perceives that life is trying to break him, does he abandon himself. In the asylum of Berlin-Buch, Death speaks plainly with Franz who now, at last, no longer tries to preserve himself. For it was Death that sent him all the blows, that had spoken continuously to him, that Franz always ran away from— until the end:

Yes, you were right, Franz, in coming to me. How can man prosper if he does not seek Death? Death, true and real. You preserved yourself all your life. To preserve, to preserve—that is man's terrible desire, and thus it stays in one spot, and it can't go on that way. (AB, 599)

Franz's error was that he too strongly believed in himself and his own strength and did not doubt himself:

It never entered your head to blame yourself and everything you had undertaken. You clung to force with might and main, and the spasm continues to reign, and it's no use, you realize it yourself, no use whatever; the moment comes, and vain is all endeavor. Death does not sing a gentle song for you, nor does he place a strangling necklace around your throat. I am life and truest strength, and now at last, at last, you will preserve yourself no longer. (AB, 600)

The paradox of the last sentence is only understandable in the light of Döblin's philosophy of nature. Death is life, that is, it is the power that destroys the formed and form-conscious individual which, in Döblin's conviction, death clings to, and death leads him back to the world of the anonymous, which alone is eternal. Franz's misfortune is clearly derived from his false claim on the world, which he now ruefully acknowledges. The positive aspect of his strength is that he survives; once again he stands on the Alexanderplatz, but he is no longer alone, for "much unhappiness comes from walking alone. When there are several, it's somewhat different" (AB, 633). Franz's guilt is his imagined strength, his attempt to survive the world alone. In the end, Biberkopf realizes that he must join up with others, with the *right* fellow men. The political-social dimension of the novel becomes clear at this point. Döblin's socialism is inseparable from his philosophy of nature, the greater importance, the deeper truth lies for him with the masses. Nonetheless, the twist at the end of the novel has confused most critics. But it comes by no means unexpectedly, for in one of the many political discussions which Franz becomes involved in, an anarchist worker tries to explain to him that alone he is powerless. Finally, Franz declares self-assuredly: "A man's got only himself, just himself. I look after myself. I'm a self-provider, I am!" The worker replies: "And I've told you that three dozen times already: you can't do anything alone. We need a fighting organization. . . . You don't know what

Mythology and Modern Existence

is the most important thing for the proletariat: solidarity" (AB, 373).

But, as always, Franz disregards this appeal, too. Only at the end does he recognize the necessity for solidarity, a solidarity whose platform must first be subjected to a test because Franz has been burnt once. The novel ends with a vision of the revolutionary masses marching into a war of liberation—a surprising turn which is, however, connected to Biberkopf's earlier mistaken attitude and thus seems justified. It is to be assumed that the events of the time could have determined Döblin to force this consequence from Franz's fate.

Nonetheless, the activist ending stands in a certain opposition to the theme of sacrifice dominant in the novel: having learned self-abandonment from his fate, Biberkopf appears in the ambiguous ending as one marching with the revolutionary masses which seek to determine their own fate. This ending has the appearance of an afterthought. Döblin saw the inherent dualism in it—it is this dualism which is the basis of all his thought and which appears here in a stronger political—social illumination. He defended himself against these charges by asserting that the end was to be a transition to a second volume depicting the active man, if not the same person—a book which was never written. Döblin himself discloses that his philosophy of nature is more important than political considerations when he writes:

A more passive-receptive element with a tragic cast is placed against an active element which is more optimistic—the "Ich in der Natur" ("self in nature") against the "Ich über der Natur" ("self above nature"). In *Berlin Alexanderplatz*, I really wanted to bring Franz Biberkopf to the second phase,—I failed. Against my will, simply by the logic of the action and of the plan, the book ended in this way; it was not to be saved. I was bitterly disappointed. The ending really should have played in heaven, another soul saved, well that was impossible, but I didn't let it stop me from having fanfares at the end, whether it was psychologically correct or not. Up to now I see: dualism cannot be stopped.[21]

These remarks also reveal the political dilemma in which Döblin found himself in these years of the growing Fascist threat.[22] He was convinced that action was needed but, at the same time, he could not overcome his skepticism toward action.

CHAPTER 7

"Why Write, and for Whom?"[1]
The Novels of the Exile

BEFORE political events forced him to leave Germany, Döblin published three additional works. In *Unser Dasein* (1933; "Our Existence") he develops, once again, his philosophy of nature on a wider basis without arriving at any conclusions which go beyond *Das Ich über der Natur*. Esthetic observations, which add nothing essentially new, and observations about the fate of the Jewish people and Judaism are included. The drama *Die Ehe* (1931; "Marriage") is a play of social criticism which treats the problems of marriage on three different social levels, a theme which Döblin takes up again in *Pardon wird nicht gegeben* (trsl. 1937; *Men without Mercy*). The play uses the techniques of epic theater as Piscator developed them for his political theater and Brecht for his didactic plays. And, last but not least, Döblin's most important political essay, *Wissen und Verändern!* (1931), summing up his convictions in political and social matters, was published. This work has already been discussed in an earlier chapter.

Although his output during the period of exile was steady—despite the adverse external circumstances—he did not achieve the quality of his earlier works. Therefore many studies of his *oeuvre* are limited to the years prior to 1933. The reasons for this obvious loss of quality can only be guessed. Repeated complaints in Döblin's letters bear witness to his suffering from the language barrier and to his feeling of separation from the native soil. There was also, of course, the lack of a large German library of the kind on which he always relied for preparation of his epic works. Philosophical reasons were, however, more important. Since Döblin's world view was oriented toward a distinct philosophy of nature, his image of man must have been shaken by

[110]

"Why Write, and for Whom?"

the enormous catastrophe which had broken over Germany and the world. What did his repeatedly postulated—if precarious—harmony of man and nature mean in the face of these political upheavals? Indeed, hadn't he involuntarily and indirectly contributed to the rise of Fascism by treating the theme of submission? Was he not collectively guilty? All the old bonds were ruptured. Unable to bear complete bondlessness, Döblin, whose metaphysical need and demand for public esteem appears early in his life, sought desperately for new bonds. The unclear confession of guilt, a desperate seeking for answers and, since these were not forthcoming, a stubborn clinging to sham solutions now forced their way so much into the foreground of his works that their structure often lacks coherence and plasticity. The books written after 1933 offer shocking proof of the crisis and the dilemma faced by the author, but they are hardly works of high artistic value.[2]

I Babylonische Wandrung

In his autobiographical report (*Schicksalsreise*), Döblin depicted the genesis and the theme of the first novel he wrote mostly in exile. It first appeared in 1934 in the Exil-Verlag Querido in Amsterdam:

In 1932, a strange image implanted itself in me. I didn't understand its meaning: an ancient, moldy god leaves his heavenly home before the beginning of the end; a sinister sentence from which he cannot exempt himself, forces him to eath. He must expiate his old sins. (Sr, 395 f.)

In Döblin's opinion, this was the great feeling of guilt and the repudiation of the profounder experience he had already had at his disposal. The experience to which Döblin alludes is that of the necessity of sacrifice and humility. To a certain extent, the novel *Babylonische Wandrung* ("Babylonian Migration") is an ironic treatment of the theme of *Berlin Alexanderplatz*:

This book, *Babylonische Wandrung*, made fun, in a terrible way, of the idea of sacrifice as broached in *Alexanderplatz*. The god Konrad does not think at all of expiation; he does not even feel dethroned, deposed, and he retains this attitude. I just don't know how my plan slipped away from me as I wrote.[3]

Here we have, then, a relation similar to that between *Wang-lun* and *Wadzek*.

The narrative method used in *Babylonische Wandrung* is far removed from the collage technique of *Berlin Alexanderplatz*. In its course, the story concentrates on the fate of the chief figures, especially of Konrad, so that the obtrusion of thematic elements is reinforced by formal aspects, as mentioned above. The spiritual experience of the individual is thrust more forcefully into view than the total reality which surrounds, and acts on, the individual. From another point of view, Döblin remained faithful to himself; even in *Babylonische Wandrung*, "epic appositions" dominate the narrative structure. But, to be sure, Döblin quite readily gave in to his weakness to illuminate human error ironically and satirically in these digressions. The unity of the novel frequently suffers from this shortcoming.

The god Marduk, whom the narrator here prefers to call Konrad, sees himself driven out of his Babylonian heaven by the curse of a certain Jeremias, for the sacrifical odors which nourish him fail to reach him. The novel then depicts his "lusty and dolorous way through all the humanness of drink, of love, of earning money, until he becomes a poor little man."[4]

Konrad has been sent to earth, not only to become acquainted with humanity in its lusty and terrible aspects, but also to expiate a sin at first only vaguely defined. Characteristically, it is that of pride, as the subtitle shows: *Oder Hochmut kommt vor dem Fall* ("Pride goeth before the Fall"). Konrad is not at all aware of his failing, and continues in his pride and arrogance. He holds fast to his claim to godliness and at first tries only to regain his lost position. Clearly, in this picture Döblin ironically attacks the claim to sovereignty by the individual who feels autonomous. Konrad is not ready to stop resisting, to surrender himself, or to abandon his own individuality to the irrationality and totality of life.

Georg, another character, is also cast out of heaven, and later Old Man Waldemar becomes the third member of their band. Konrad stands between the well-known extremes embodied in these figures. The quiet, friendly Waldemar, with his devotion to alcohol, embodies passivity, while Georg is a cynic of power and coercion—a barb aimed at the new power holders in Germany. It is no mere coincidence that he reminds us of Reinhold and

"Why Write, and for Whom?"

Wallenstein. Georg develops into a hardened criminal, and at his expense Konrad lives quite well. His activities often bring him into contact with the police, thus motivating numerous changes of scene: Baghdad, Constantinople, Paris, with Zurich and Strasbourg as way stations.

Despite all sorts of humiliating experiences, and despite many admonishments from the narrator, Konrad remains essentially unshaken. He does not want to accept the fate of being a simple, little man. Only in Constantinople does he comprehend more fully the ambivalence of human existence: he experiences on the one hand the boundless isolation of the individual, his mortality and fragility, and on the other the joyous feeling of being carried by the stream of life—an antithesis that is traceable through all of Döblin's work. It is no coincidence that his tragic love affair with the Russian woman, Alexandra—thus, once again, love and death—opens a more profound understanding of existence for him. She becomes his "eye opener" (BW, 412). Konrad wants nothing more than to be a man with his ups and downs; however, he is not spared from relapses into his former arrogance.

Konrad's experiences seem always to pose the same question: should he—like Waldemar—be satisfied with a vegetative, passive existence, seeking only pleasure and joy; or are force, might, and money the only effective agents in this world—as Georg continuously tries to prove to him? Can people act, can they change anything? Konrad feels both sides of human nature in himself, but cannot decide for either. Even in death Waldemar smiles peacefully, being reconciled with his life; Georg, on the other hand, is depicted—in a digression—at a macabre military parade. He is finally described as a devil who says of himself: "I am the spoiler" (BW, 492).

In Strasbourg, Konrad mixes in with the medieval parade of flagellants, which the narrator conjures up anachronistically: the longing for the salvation of man is eternal, but so are his cruelty and his hatred. The flagellants are marching to kill Strasbourg's Jewry. In purifying and healing pain, Konrad burns, with them—that, too, is a familiar motif. Yet he burns in vain, for he still is senseless stone; he is not dissolved and does not return to the anonymity of all-powerful nature—at least not yet. In Zurich, love and birth, and with them the recognition of the self-perpetuating endlessness of life, are the things that become important for Konrad. Religion remains meaningless for him; he refuses to accept the theses of Balthasar, the theology student and disciple of Zwingli, regarding the guilt and damnation of man. Once again Konrad denies all guilt; he is what he is—how can he, then, be guilty? Yet in Konrad's unstable psychic structure the crisis is always latent. Back in Paris he is only apparently the same old epicurean, for the recognition of mortality, isolation, and impotence strikes him with unexpected rapidity. Behind the back of his antihero, as it were, the narrator conjures up death and the suffering Christ, who are hidden behind the smiles of the city and the beauty of its churches.

By a trick, Konrad is deprived of the financial support provided by Georg's activity. He has to spend his nights on the Metro steps among the clochards where, however, he soon feels at home—like many of Döblin's heroes—among the nameless, the poor, the oppressed, and the outcast of society. Now that Konrad has hit rock bottom, he is ready to abandon himself. But Georg saves him from this situation and makes one last attempt to win Konrad over to his own world view. He shows him "Menschlistadt," a parody city inhabited by sheep: the people are numbered among the dumb animals and must be ordered about and exploited.

Konrad is not convinced; what Georg has to show him is, in his view, merely the "world as a horror picture" (BW, 601). Although he sees force at work everywhere, he still senses that the very successful Georg is wrong. In the face of all appearances, he intuitively believes in justice. These contradictions now occur more and more openly and are an eloquent proof of the crisis in which Döblin found himself. Konrad reproaches God, his successor in power, for having given man the power to think and feel, but not simultaneously the power to act. He sees himself as a powerless toy in the hands of a cynical god whom he curses. But at the same time, he offers to help God free the world from its being so terrible. He sees the futility of the world but believes that he feels its sense. He negates the possibility of action, and yet he wants to help; he understands the powerlessness of the individual and still believes that he has the power to tame evil, for he tries to chain Georg again—as once in his Babylonian heaven. He believes that there is justice, for why else would they have been sent to earth? He also knows that Georg is as immortal

"Why Write, and for Whom?"

as Christ, and that he himself shares in both of them.

Konrad's impotence and weakness are attested by his failure to carry out his noble plan to chain Georg up again: Konrad "dodges, remains a parasite" (BW, 621). Here again one of the key words from *Berlin Alexanderplatz* surfaces. Konrad once more takes money from Georg, marries, has children, and leads the life of a wealthy pensioner. He sees Georg, "the marching battalions" (BW, 650), ruling everywhere and withdraws from the cities from which nothing good can come. He flees with his family to a bucolic idyll in Southern France. Here, in contact with the soil he finally surrenders himself completely; he returns—as do nearly all of Döblin's figures—to the primeval powers, and gives himself back to them. Dying, he realizes that "a great leadership" (BW, 665) permeates the world. The adjuration of the unity of man and nature, which could still be understood in *Berge Meere und Giganten* as a counterbalance against machine-age destruction in a great historical cycle, has here only the effect of an evasion, as a resigned retreat into an artificial idyll. After Konrad's experiences, after his persistent questioning, after all the unconcealed allusions to the present, this ending, based on Döblin's philosophy of nature, is rather incredible. Nonetheless, Döblin's philosophy of nature is still the continuous and stable element in his thought; and in the face of his desperate situation, one can see why he will cling to it further as the one thing that supports him. Having just arrived in exile, Döblin reasserted the dominant role of his idea of the superego in a letter to Paul Fechter referring to his book *Unser Dasein:* "It is the great true formative ego which is always my point of departure, and the perception of its whole nature and expansion is my constantly renewed task."[5]

II Pardon wird nicht gegeben

Döblin repeatedly stressed that he was especially strongly influenced by the literature of the North and of the East. His relationship to French literature was rather cool; he knew, among others, Flaubert, Balzac, Stendhal, Baudelaire, Anatole France, Romain Rolland, and Bernanos, all of whom he showed little enthusiasm for; he had also studied Proust. But now, as an exile who made an effort to learn the language and literature of his host country, he rediscovered French literature and entered into a more productive relationship with it. He read heavily but unselectively in Pascal, Corneille, and Stendhal. "I am learning French, and I am seeking bridges to this other culture; it is better, clearer, and more mundane than German culture. But I was not a German and will not become a Frenchman," he wrote in 1934.[6] Apparently, the novel *Pardon wird nicht gegeben* (*Men without Mercy*, trsl. by Traver and Phyllis Blewitt, London, 1937; literal meaning, "Pardon will not be granted"), his "family history with an autobiographical admixture,"[7] was influenced by his reading of the great French nineteenth-century novelists, for it is written in a conventional style and is diametrically opposed to Döblin's notion of an epic work.

As no other novel before it, *Babylonische Wandrung* exposed the antinomies in Döblin's thought: What could be more appropriate now than to see in *Pardon wird nicht gegeben* a retreat into his personal history. But such an interpretation surely fails to do justice to the novel. Like Edward Allison in his subsequent novel, *Hamlet*, Döblin is hunting for guilt, his own as well as that of society. The question of guilt would also be the point of departure for his trilogy about the unsuccessful German revolution of 1918. Thus we have only an apparent retreat into autobiography. In truth, Döblin uses autobiographical material to study the sins of the past which are responsible for the catastrophe of the present.

The autobiographical point of departure is unmistakably the collapse of Döblin's family and his move to Berlin. But the five children are reduced to three: Karl, the oldest (a mask for Döblin's older brother Ludwig), Erich, and little Marie who, however, soon dies. The misery, debts, and desperation of the mother are so great that she tries to commit suicide but is saved by Karl. From this moment, she pursues her own rise in society, and that of her son, with thoroughness and perseverance. Roaming through the streets in search of work and income, Karl meets the precocious, young social revolutionary, Paul. Döblin modeled this figure on the young lyric poet, Hugo Lyck, an early Berlin acquaintance, whose humanity had impressed him so much that he remembered him even much later.[8] Paul shows him the misery of the proletariat in the big city and opens his eyes to the bourgeoisie—the class from which Karl's mother has fallen and to

"Why Write, and for Whom?"

which she is now seeking to return by hook or by crook. In naïve trust of his admired friend, Karl believes that he can only remain a good man and preserve his humanity if he turns his back on the bourgeoisie and follows Paul. He is prepared to—indeed, wants to—steal his mother's badly needed money to convince Paul of the earnestness of his decision to follow him. But his mother stops the execution of the plan and forces him to obey her and to accept her plans for his future. In place of the spouse, who has deserted her, she relies on her oldest son. A threefold crime has taken place: the crime of the mother against her son, his crime against himself, and his betrayal of society.

Much earlier, Karl's mother had decided to place Karl in her brother's furniture factory. Karl sides with the workers, and in order to avoid promotion he begins to sabotage his work; but in vain. His resistance is permanently broken by his mother. From now on, Karl plays the role that bourgeois society outlines for him: he makes a career, becomes director of the factory, and, since his role prescribes it, he marries the daughter of a high official—a choice also made for him by his mother. Social conventions replace any personal relationship between the spouses. His connection with Paul and his hatred of bourgeois society are now only youthful aberrations for him. He has had to pay for his social rise with the loss of his integrity and individuality.

Karl's life runs like a clock—but only as long as the boom lasts. The foundations of his external existence are shaken by the beginning world economic crisis. In search of her own individual existence, his wife breaks out of the role forced upon her and, taking her two children, she moves in with a lover. This movement on the individual level is repeated, on the social level, by the collapse of Karl's bourgeois existence. He must recognize the corruption not only in the bourgeoisie but also in the nobility which the bourgeoisie had held in awe. Karl, himself a social climber, has gone too far and is dropped by his own class. His financial difficulties continue to grow.

Now, liberated by the crisis which has exposed his illusory existence, the elementary power of unlived life breaks out of him in full force. But this repressed power cannot speak the language of society; it is therefore speechless, confused, and wild. It drives him to the outskirts of the city, to whores who accept him as an individual, as a human being, and do not ask where he comes from or what he does. Like so many of Döblin's figures, Karl, too, flees into anonymity. Here he is only a human being; despite his external degeneration, he finds his earlier, better self again. He tries to attach himself to Paul, who has returned to the city as an agitator, to justify and heal himself. Although Paul retreats to a class-struggle position, and an understanding between the two is impossible, Karl finds himself again under the influence of conversations with his former friend. He recognizes the necessity of revolution and is ready to stand at Paul's side.

Yet his end is ironic: he happens upon a patrol of civil defensemen, members of an organization which he himself helped establish. In his attempt to join the rebels and thus to complete his change externally, he is shot down and honored as a martyr by the class he was trying to escape from. Even in death his class does not release its hold on him.

Although Döblin makes extensive use of his brother's fate here, (he had committed suicide), he projected his own conflicts and guilt feelings into this figure. His ambivalent relationship to his mother as preserver and tyrant is evident. she was the one who persuaded him to marry Erna Reiss. Powerless and vain rebellion against mother and wife characterize these relationships and are rather openly mirrored in the book.

No less important than these intimate conflicts uncovered in the novel is its statement regarding the author's social position. Although Döblin always stressed that he belonged to the poor, he made, under the influence of a family that had become bourgeois again, a good match, while a poor girl had a child by him. He practiced a bourgeois profession, albeit in a poor area, and socialized in bourgeois circles. Thus, despite his definite antibourgeois attitude, he had strong ties to the middle class. It seems almost like a secret confession of guilt when Karl—against his better desires and judgment—is caught in the bourgeois sphere after his rebellion against it has been repressed by his mother.

At this point, the autobiographical perspective touches upon the historical one. The novel ends with a vision of the unsuccessful revolution of 1918, which was to be the subject of Döblin's longest book. He had been an eyewitness to the conquest of the Berlin suburb of Lichtenberg by the reactionary troops. Döblin's sister, Meta, was killed during these revolutionary dis-

"Why Write, and for Whom?"

turbances when she tried to get milk for her children. In Döblin's view, the truly revolutionary forces were suppressed by a coalition of the moderate Social Democrats and the old reactionary and military circles. Thus this unsuccessful revolution—at least, as Döblin saw it—was the source of the impending catastrophic development. The novel *Pardon wird nicht gegeben* describes how a member of the bourgeoisie, who should have known better from his own experience, does not dare to join the revolutionary movement at the right time. Thus, half intentionally, he betrays the incipient social order to the resurrected military and noble circles. The novel converges completely with Döblin's political thinking and the description of the revolution in *November 1918*.

But as in all of Döblin's novels, here, too, we have a contrast figure. It is Karl's younger brother, the lazy, passive Erich, who lives at peace with himself. He houses revolutionaries, sympathizes with them, but does not openly or actively support them. He lives, as it were, in the shadow of a fate which, because of his passivity, he does not challenge. And he has the last word in the novel; of him it is said—reminiscent of *Wang-lun*—: "He lived very quietly" (Pard, 370). Basically an unpolitical figure, to whom humaneness is more important than his career and the daily political battle, he displays the other side of Döblin's character, i.e., the attempt to keep things universally human out of partisan squabbles in order to preserve them; an attempt that—as we have seen—was condemned to failure.

While Karl is challenged to join the revolution, meeting this challenge too late, Erich—again very typically for Döblin—marks the opposite position. He lives a peaceful life and abstains from direct political activities. Thus, once more, Döblin's skepticism toward action is integrated into the novel.

III Amazonas

In his work, Döblin was always dependent on libraries. In 1935, in the Bibliothèque Nationale in Paris, he happened to come across some atlases which distracted him from his studies of Kierkegaard.[9] Here he rediscovered something that had always fascinated him: immeasurable nature and, especially, water, i.e., the Amazon river, "this miracle, river-ocean, a thing of prehistory."[10] It acted as the stimulus for his South American trilogy. The novel *Amazonas* ("The Amazon") appeared in 1937 and 1938 and consisted of two volumes: *Die Fahrt ins Land ohne Tod* (1937; "The Journey into the Land without Death") and *Der blaue Tiger* (1938; "The Blue Tiger"). After the war, a second edition of the work appeared (in 1947 and 1948) under the title *Das Land ohne Tod. Südamerika-Roman in drei Teilen* ("The Land without Death. South American Novel in Three Parts"). Döblin cut off the last part of the novel and published it by itself under the title *Der neue Urwald* (1948; "The New Primeval Forest").[11]

The life of the Indians and Indian myths soon fascinated him as much as the boundless nature of South America, as is shown by the titles of the individual volumes. He then depicted the brutal conquest of South America by the Spaniards, material that he had become acquainted with through Gerhart Hauptmann's *Der weisse Heiland*. Döblin discussed that play in *Der deutsche Maskenball* and criticized it severely; in contrast to Hauptmann, he took the side of the conqueror Cortez, not that of the passive Montezuma.[12] However, in the novel the situation is quite different because Döblin clearly sympathizes with the indigenous population.

At the center of the trilogy is "the grandiose attempt of humanity," the founding of the Jesuit Republic on the Parana.[13] The general theme of the book is, in Döblin's words,

> the struggle between the idea (the mere idea) "god" and the concrete reality and genuine truth: nature. Therefore the life of the Indians is protrayed, the old empire of the Amazons. This part is followed by the invasion of the Whites into the little known empire Cundinamarka (Bolivia). Then the Jesuit state Paraguay is founded as a Christian Republic, and its final disintegration is depicted. A final European chapter closes the work.[14]

The world of water and of forests is peopled by Indians who live in harmony with nature and humbly venerate its powers, for only in this manner can they survive. They exist in a condition of natural innocence in which they can drive away neither the brutal, greedy conquistadores, whose motives and ways of doing things they really do not understand, nor the Jesuits. Passively they submit to the context of life to which they belong. After the natural order has been temporarily disturbed, as in the battle of

"Why Write, and for Whom?"

the Amazons against the men—once again the motif of the sexes is sounded—all returns to the harmony of the original condition. Many of those who enter here—including the conquistadores—cannot withstand the magic of this paradisiacal life, and they succumb to the Indian way of life by beginning to imitate it.

In spite of their desire for passive submission to nature, the conquistadores are marked by the most uninhibited and most brutal activity which, aroused by their lust for gold, always jars them out of their inclination to passive submission. In vain, Cuzumarra has tried to warn his people against the terrible intruders and to mobilize the tribes against them. The conquistadores have come "to destroy and to lose themselves" (Am, 94); they arrive in the land "like a sickness in a body" (Am, 179). The ravages of war, misanthropy, and greed proceed their march as allegorical figures. Their senseless, brutal life calls forth a similar death. Almost to a man, they are devoured by immeasurable nature.

The conquistadores, who have been loosed upon the continent for political and economic reasons, are not the only Whites who penetrate that far. "Europe, the cramped, unhappy continent, also had other men. There were those who sought more sincerely and were not chased, who intended to do penance and to reveal the true face of the white man" (Am, 421). They left a Europe in which the Reformation and religious wars were dominant and in which Christianity had failed. They came to make a new start in South America, and had not only to fight against the primeval forest. The title of the third book of the first part of the novel makes that quite clear: "Las Casas und Sukuruja"—the Jesuit priest and the spirit of water, i.e., of the Amazon. Since the dark men are constantly confronted with the discrepancy between the theory and practice of Christianity in the white man's camp, Las Casas goes to their home in the primeval forest. In his visionary dream, in which he travels to Spain with the Indians and demands that the Christian king step down from his throne, the reversal of the missionary course takes place: it is no longer the Indian "heathens" (who have preserved an original, unbroken humanity) who need to be converted, but the white "Christians," who do not exemplify the humane spirit of their religion, but continuously violate it. Las Casas experiences the magic and unison of nature, a proof to him of how miraculously God has made the world. Unlike the other figures in the novel he does not completely succumb to nature. His mission fails because of the baseness of the Whites, whom he cannot completely avoid. After one of their evil deeds, Las Casas is killed by the Indians; dying, he falls on the cross and rosary, and thus even in death he firmly holds on to the symbols of his religion.

Following the structural principle Döblin had developed in *Berge Meere und Giganten,* namely to present the basic conflict (here religion vs. nature) in the close juxtaposition of a prelude in order to take it up again and expand it in a larger context, he now depicts the founding and decay of the Jesuit Republic over several generations. In the second part (*Der blaue Tiger*), however, nature and the myths of nature move into the background, in favor of the portrayal of the fate of a theocratic state. The attempt to found a Christian Republic fails. The Jesuits think that they can seal themselves off and withdraw into isolation by avoiding São Paolo, the center of the evil brought upon them by the Whites. In so doing, they break the law of interdependence of all things. The first settlement, "the Indian Canaan" (Am, 365), has to be abandoned because of attacks from São Paolo. The new settlement, repeating the "peaceful life of the simple fishermen on the Sea of Galilee" (Am, 424) and the site of Biblical miracles, is destroyed by a ridiculous usurper. The end of the last settlement is finally brought about by a political agreement between Spain and Portugal in which the Jesuits are mere objects. The Age of Absolutism begins without any place being assigned to the Jesuits.

Not only the activity of the criminals in São Paolo and the political machinations, but also the immensity of nature constitute a constant danger. Repeatedly, individuals succumb to the life of the Indians. Thus Father Mariana dances into the woods with them and is swallowed up by the elements. Even Emanuel, the chief of the first Jesuit Republic—as witnessed by his profound spiritual tie to the former chieftain's wife Maladonata—is by no means free from the inclination to which Mariana has completely surrendered.

For the paradox of the situation results from the Indians not only embodying a more beautiful and perfect humanity but also from their being free, in Döblin's view, from the spiritual torments of the Whites. Christian teachings are fulfilled by the dark

"Why Write, and for Whom?"

ones in a very elemental sense because in their pure humanness they are much closer to the maxims of the Christian life in its original meaning than are the Christian themselves—and thus their conversion is really superfluous. They are untouched particularly by one aspect of the teachings, that of sacrifice and suffering:

> The dark men who entrusted themselves to the Jesuits belonged to this part of the earth and grew on it. They followed the new magical teaching of a ruler over the animals, trees, over the spirits and births, and of a savior. No breath of the suffering and spiritual torment from which the foreign teaching was born touched them. (Am, 478 f)

Thus the Jesuits want to renew the teaching and reaffirm it from their point of view: "Christianity tried to save itself from its white followers through the dark ones" (Am, 468 f.). But the chasm between the natural humanness of the Indians and the unnaturalness of the Whites is unbridgeable—a return to the original harmony with nature has become impossible; the process of human history is irreversible.

Even so, the theocratic republic has a utopian aspect: "The state of God, the grandiose attempt, the only one worthy of man, begun by Father Emanuel, had failed" (Am, 616). The undertaking fails not merely because of the reasons familiar from Döblin's other writings, such as the isolation or arrogance of the leaders, but also because it comes too late. Döblin aligns the demise of the Jesuit Republic with the great historical turning point, the Renaissance, in which man runs away from the other world and toward this world. In the struggle between God and nature, the latter seems to win in the end. The new discoveries of natural science were understood by the Indians who live in an idealized natural context and follow the laws of nature instinctively by virtue of their more profound understanding of it. Their passive alignment, however, is contrasted with the active natural science originating with the Renaissance, which results in the domination of nature. This return to earth, by means of which men hoped to renew themselves "at a source that is no less deep and holy than that of the church" (Am, 620) is greeted as a good omen. Döblin seems to want to rest firmly on the home ground of his "naturalism."

But for this very reason, the third part of the trilogy (*Der neue Urwald*), suppressed by Walter Muschg in his edition, is so important. It shows that this returning to earth does not work toward the salvation of man. Autobiographically, it demonstrates that all Döblin's suprapersonal views of human relationships have been shaken. His philosophy of nature has been shaken because a true harmony of the white man with nature seems impossible; the way back to paradisiacal innocence, lost because of man's desire for knowledge and activity, is blocked. Any practical religiosity has been shaken because the Christianity of the conquistadores is a farce, and because the attempt to found a theocratic state, seemingly worthy of man, but anachronistic and a flight from the reality of the white race, fails, like all great political undertakings in Döblin's works. Finally, even Döblin's "naturalism" that has not produced the hoped-for renewal of man by association with the earth, but rather has produced an extremely ambivalent result, has been shaken: "The new earth had made them feel good, but had also raised their power, their pride, and their crudeness and increased their unhappiness" (DnU, 5). No wonder that Döblin wrote about the last part: "The denouement (*Abgesang*) of this South American work (*Der neue Urwald*) cannot avoid showing the terrible, hopeless, brooding deprivation which is left behind."[15]

As in *Berge Meere und Giganten*, the new devotion to earth does not lead to a more perfect humanity, but to hubris as it is found in Fascism, where a particular type of man makes himself the measure of all things.

The thematic problem of the *Neue Urwald*, which, as far as subject matter is concerned, is only loosely connected with the other two parts, leads to the radical formulation of the question of whether this world is meaningful, interwoven with providence, or whether it is chaotic. The conversation between Twardowski, the Polish Faust, on the one side, and Kepler, Galileo, and Giordano Bruno—one of Döblin's favorites—on the other, deals precisely with this question. That the conversation is set in the Church of St. Mary in Cracow is surely not only determined by the figure of Twardowski: in this church Döblin experienced, as we have seen, a kind of religious ecstasy. For Twardowski the world is chaotic and evil, and he accuses Kepler and Galileo of having founded the godless world. Despite Twardowski's con-

"Why Write, and for Whom?"

traditions, Bruno affirms his perceptions and praises the glory of the world in phrases that are strongly reminiscent of *Das Ich über der Natur*. He does not doubt that the world is guided by "the connection to a highest intelligence" (DnU, 12). Although he realizes that man's misfortune stems from his overabundance of power, he believes in the possibility of a new humanity and praises the creative power of man. Twardowski counters: "No. In this world nothing happens. Everything just moves" (DnU, 14). The fates presented in this last part serve as illustrations of this antithesis.

Klinkert and his friend, Posten, pay homage to sobriety, strength, and power; their symbol is the machine. They oppose all mythology and demand factual methods. As a sign of this "instrumental thinking," Klinkert always carries a small nickel scissors around with him. But as so often in Döblin, Klinkert's arrogance and cynicism, his glorification of power and force are broken by the decisive phenomena of life: love and death. Therese's love and her suicide shake his Fascist ideology to its foundations and lead him to the realization of his own nothingness and of the absurdity of the world:

Hellish, satanic world! The scorn of everything we are and would like to be. Therese lying on her face, every bone in her body smashed. No pity, no one intervenes. We are defenseless and alone. (DnU, 114)

For Twardowski, Klinkert's fate is only one more proof that there is no reason, wisdom, and love in the world. Even Bruno admits that he has seen a "disfigured humanity" (DnU, 122). Evil has taken control of his perceptions as well as that of the others. For him there remains only the utopian hope: the old humanity shall be destroyed—in typically Expressionistic fashion—and a new and better one created. What he has seen in Klinkert's fate, he can—as so often in Döblin—grasp only by means of a paradox: "Oh disfigured world! Oh glorious earth!" (DnU, 124). Klinkert's fate remains uncertain, and the close of his life (not of the book) reflects life's cul-de-sac. The political development of Fascism, organically linked to the ideology earlier associated with Klinkert, strengthens his despair. The only thing left for the disillusioned Klinkert is the intuition of a supraindividual ego. Timorously,

Döblin re-invokes the basic idea of his philosophy of nature, but this time without real conviction:

The self. It is the self. Perhaps not our self, as we imagine it. Perhaps another, stronger, more powerful self that has something in it, wants something, doesn't want something—that knows what it wants. (DnU, 143)

The story of Klinkert is interpolated with that of Jagna; the two are loosely connected. Jagna goes through a process similar to Klinkert's: in the beginning, he is a misanthrope of boundless cynicism, especially in his relations with women. But soon he realizes the senselessness of his activities:

There is nothing that holds us. You just drift about. I could just keep drifting around. You know how far that's gotten me. It's no fun any more. I shudder at continuing, and I don't know anything but to continue. (DnU, 55)

Like so many of Döblin's figures, Jagna disappears in anonymity; he walks a self-appointed *via dolorosa*. Klinkert finally finds him again as a simple working man in Paris when he (Jagna) is about to go to the Bagno in Guinea with a friend convicted of murder and the latter's girl friend. He is turning his back on Europe and its people, from whom he expects nothing more. "There remains only the possibility of demolishing everything here or of going away" (DnU, 135). The cultural pessimism repeatedly surfacing in this trilogy, but already evident earlier, is most radically expressed here; but that is not to say that Jagna is definitely Döblin's mouthpiece.

Restless, Jagna leaves the Bagno too; he flees with a group of convicts through the primeval jungle to Brazil. In this way, the narrator returns to the setting of the other parts of the trilogy. In the end, only Jagna and a half-mad deacon are left. In the conversations they have with the Indians, the horrors of Europe are once again confronted by the natural, plantlike life of the Indians. For the latter, the world of the Whites is one of barbarity and violence, from which only disorder results. Thus again Western civilization is criticized and condemned through the eyes of the Indians. According to their mythological ideas, the great father has sent the blue tiger to earth to destroy the countries of the Whites. Having perceived the senselessness of action, the two survivors lose themselves more and more in the world of the Indians. Jagna falls in love with an Indian girl, who becomes for him the symbol of the maternal powers of life—in contrast to the destructive masculine principle. He dies among the Indians, while the deacon dies in the primeval forest.

In the last sections of the book, Döblin praises, once again, the great maternal powers of life and of nature—probably more from the need to frame the extremely disparate, contradictory, and irridescent whole than from any inner logic. Sukuruja joyfully views the dance of her children into destruction. They are looking for paradise in order to escape from a world of force and destruction brought on by the Whites—thus with increasing urgency the desire for salvation is expressed in Döblin's books.

The novel demonstrates, above all, how questionable Döblin's religion of nature had become to him, a religion—as he himself repeatedly stressed—which he considered to be the center of his works. The vacuum that resulted from the shaking of his belief in his philosophy of nature had to be filled again—by the Christian religion which Döblin now finally approached and fused with his philosophy of nature. The figure of Christ is by no means absent from his earlier works, but there it is a secularized symbol of human sacrifice and suffering—a contrast symbol to Prometheus:

I see Christ as a contrast figure to ancient Prometheus. Prometheus brought fire to earth, brought man out of the caves and made him ruler over some of the forces of nature. To be Promethean is human majesty; not to understand the limits of the Promethean is human folly. (Sr, 182)[16]

At first, the other idea had been incomprehensible to him: that this true symbol of human existence is God himself descended to human life. Döblin grows closer and closer to this belief.

IV November 1918

Döblin's process of conversion was accelerated by the profound spiritual crisis precipitated by the flight through France, especially in the refugee camp of Mende and in the local cathedral. Attempting a radical inventory of his life in the face of this existential crisis, he held fast to the basic idea of his philosophy of nature, but tried to link it with the concept of a personal god:

And "Jesus" is not a god of "addition," no revision of existence, but (I speculate) an adjunct to our clear understanding of what existence and the world really are. Even in this disintegrated world, clarity means the primeval basis, which has carried us upwards, has not lost its relation to Him. Do we feel lost? We must not believe that we are lost, mere, dull "individuals." Jesus says: the world is bad, but it has a history, and we have a fate which extends beyond earthly existence. (Sr, 213)

In his later religious books, most clearly in *Der unsterbliche Mensch* ("Immortal Man"), Döblin also follows up this train of thought: the Christian religion is not simply to replace his philosophy of nature, but it serves as the capstone of his philosophical system. These thoughts do not suddenly appear, but were—as has been shown—developed over a long period.

Besides this striving for a metaphysical meaning in life and the struggle for God, Döblin also attempts to find a concrete answer to the question of how this political situation, which undermined his whole existence, could arise. Again he turned to German history, this time to the most recent events. Wallenstein had the chance of giving German history a better turn, and Döblin wrote that novel during World War I. Now, shortly before, and during, World War II, he wrote a novel about another great, but also missed, opportunity in German history: the revolution of 1918.[17]

This massively conceived "narrative work" is Döblin's longest and probably least successful work. Döblin began working on it about 1938 and finished it five years later in Hollywood. Not only his flight through France, during which he carried the manuscript with him, but also his conversion lie between the beginning and the end and were not without influence on its development.[18]

Döblin wanted to do too much at one time and overtaxed his creative powers. He provided not only a detailed portrait of the months of revolution—December, 1918, —to January, 1919—largely a first-hand account that proceeds day by day, but also placed the German events in their international context, the peace parleys and the efforts of Woodrow Wilson. Although not the only setting, Berlin is the chief one of the trilogy. As always

"Why Write, and for Whom?"

in his works, Döblin wanted to provide a total, comprehensive picture of this era, and thus, in addition to the chief historic actors, there are a multitude of episodes and figures: the profiteers who exploit the turbulent times, the proletarian family, Imker, and the dramatist, Stauffer, who is intended purely as a burlesque contrast figure living in his own world. Their fates move through the novel, often interrupted, in novella-like independence. As in *Berlin Alexanderplatz*, however, there is also a multitude of fleeting individual fates which surface in the stream of the narrative and are quickly swallowed up again. In Döblin's masterpiece, there is a definite center, the fate of Biberkopf, to which everything else can and must be related. Here, Döblin additionally aligns episodes and fates which are often too broad, even though they are intertwined with one another. What is lacking is a center of integration that would organize the massive material internally and not merely—if at all—connect it externally. Thus the fate of the central figure, Friedrich Becker, Ph.D., which, in conjunction with the history of the revolution, serves as the backbone of the plot, is only loosely connected with the portrayal of political events. The changes that occur in him are symptomatic: resignation in the face of external events and retreat into inwardness. It is characteristic of the novel that the private and public political spheres have hardly any points of contact and nearly run alongside each other without touching. But that is not all: the fate of Becker concerns, if not God himself, then at least Johannes Tauler, the mystic, who is His mouthpiece,[19] as well as the devil in various guises. Döblin attempts to transcend the earthly sphere and to make the novel, at least in part, a Baroque *theatrum mundi*. But, as already stated, there is no internal center which—as in his other novels—could organize and connect the extremely heterogeneous parts:

In the comprehensive work, these two things run essentially parallel to each other and together: the tragic shipwreck of the German revolution of 1918 and the dark craving of this man [i.e., Friedrich Becker]. The question arises as to how he shall ever reach the stage of action. But this is what he wants. From where, and on what basis? He must refuse to decide. He cannot choose one from among several sandbars upon which to build his house. It becomes a divine and diabolic story. The man, Friedrich Becker, is surrounded by hallucina-

tions. He has to go through the "Gate of Terror and Despair." He stays alive. At the end, he finds himself broken and transformed into a Christian. (Depicted in volumes I and II).
He carries his newly won Christianity through the final volume (*Karl und Rosa*). Heaven and hell continue their fight for him. He degenerates externally; internally he is devoured. But—he is saved.[20]

In the earlier chapters, we have pointed out how Döblin judged the revolution whose inception he viewed from Alsace[21] but whose collapse he witnessed in Berlin. Nothing in his attitude had changed, for the arch-evil was the continued existence of the Prussian military Junker mentality which formed an alliance of convenience with the new and rather bourgeois, Social Democratic government:

In the last war they did not destroy Prussian militarism, that is, its caste, and they failed, therefore, in the main purpose of the war. They not only let Prussian militarism live, but exposed it to a strong stimulus, which was brought about by defeat. (Sr, 173)

The council of people's representatives, which first carried out the business of government, was the representative of the lower middle class, and not of the proletariat. A secret telephone line connected this government with the headquarters in Kassel, a line which plays an important role in Döblin's work. The combination of these two forces was finally successful in suppressing the real socialist-proletarian revolution.

Döblin unfolds the events of these hectic and turbulent three months in their totality. Since seemingly secondary events hide enough explosive material in them, nothing is unimportant. There is not enough space here to unravel the numerous criss-crossing strains of action.

Even though there is no doubt that Döblin's sympathies lie more on the side of the Spartacists, he is not entirely one-sided; even on the side of the true revolutionaries there is light and shadow. Although the author does not spare irony and sarcasm talking about the socialist government, especially with regard to Ebert, there are numerous occasions when he affects us as not ridiculous but tragic, a victim of the situation, and no longer its leader. Döblin's old theme of the questionableness of action is always present here.

"Why Write, and for Whom?"

The inability of the Germans to carry off a real revolution is presented with bitter irony; the action of the *Volksmarine* division, which, because it does not receive its pay, occupies the *Reichskanzlei* and locks up Ebert, turns into a farce. Everywhere, ignorance, a spirit of subjugation which, even during a revolution, finds it difficult to overstep proscriptions, and, above all, indecisiveness prevail. While profiteers carry out their shady business, the world of fashion takes its pleasures in bars and restaurants, the revolution gets talked to death; it is dissipated in many uncoordinated and contradictory single actions. There can be no question of a revolutionary uprising of the masses. Especially fatal is the hesitation of the Spartacist leaders, Karl Liebknecht and Rosa Luxemburg. Radek, Lenin's delegate, who constantly urges action, views the hesitation of these two chief actors with astonishment. While they are still waiting for the propitious moment, the initiative slips further and further away from them, until they are finally murdered by reactionary troops. That the hallucinations of Rosa Luxemburg take up so much space in the third volume must be seen as an index of her retreat into a spiritual inward sphere and as an expression of the failure of the political overthrow. "You always make revolutions with your mugs; your republic—nothing but an industrial accident!" says Franz Biberkopf (AB, 102)—a scornful and bitter commentary which, on the whole, reflects the spirit of the trilogy insofar as it is a portrait of the revolution. Döblin's bitterness during his work on the novel must have been increased even more by the conviction that the unsuccessful revolution had made Hitler's rise possible. In other words, if the revolution had been successful and had removed Prussian militarism, the Nazis would not have ruled in Germany and he would not have become an exile:

It was too simple for many people to believe that the Prussian regulation by drill and its discipline is the skeleton of Nazism, and that Nazism, on the whole, newly clothed and drilled in a new manner is Prussian militarism again. In order to understand that the old Prussian military camp was simply reopened and, after Germany, devoured half of Europe—to understand that, you apparently have to have lived near a camp and seen Nazi columns on the streets. This time, it was adapted to another form of Prussian militarism, a modern variety. The camp jailer has emancipated himself, democratized himself, and chased off the old educated officer. It is not just a coincidence that a former corporal directs the whole thing. They were carrying on the November revolution. (Sr, 172 f.)

Like all great political undertakings depicted in Döblin's works, the November revolution, this attempt to found a better and juster social order by a forceful change of society, also fails.

Friedrich Becker, on the other hand, wants to take the opposite tack: not the changing of society preceding the changing of men, but the alteration of man as the precondition for the alteration of society. As Döblin himself had refused, shortly before his emigration, to join one of the political parties, feeling that he could find true humanity only beyond partisanship, Becker refuses "to make a decision. He cannot choose between two and three sandbars to build his house on."[22] That is: for him truth is not to be found in the here and now, or in party ideologies, but only in transcendence. As so often in Döblin, Becker becomes a test figure of the Christian faith, of the possibility or impossibility of being a Christian, of striving daily for God:

The central figure of the novel strives for Him. A descent, a collapse occurs; the question of Jesus surfaces. Unbounded devotion follows.
What I experienced, what was coming, this crisis, I had experienced it intellectually before. It had been written down, sensed, pre-experienced, but not lived through. It could not be "lived through" in the imagination. There was only one possibility of continuation: to experience it. But this hero, Friedrich Becker, has progressed much further than I. (Sr, 350)

Becker follows the typical path of Döblin's heroes. Like Edward Allison in *Hamlet,* war and a wound put him in a profound crisis. The question of guilt leads him back to the question of the possibility of human action and issues in a desperate search for a transcendental meaning, nearly leading to insanity. The lifestyles of his friends, the political events, and party platforms, offer him no opportunity for finding the solution; his striving is directed toward the absolute. God and the devil struggle for his soul. And here it becomes clear how little Döblin's basic themes had changed despite his conversion. If in his earlier works he was concerned about the insight into the impotence of the individual,

"Why Write, and for Whom?"

about self-abandonment, and about the conscious and voluntary alignment of the individual human being in the comprehensive context of life and the laws of nature, here he is concerned about absolute submission to God's will. But, as always in Döblin, hubris, pride, and arrogance prevent the acceptance of this insight. Tauler, the mouthpiece of God and Becker's spiritual mentor, explains it to him:

> You high proud soul, you accept nothing as an answer except what makes you even higher and prouder. You are going through the Gate of Terror and Despair. Your pride leads you down this path. You will not find the truth in any other way. (Nov 18, II, 205)

At this point, i.e., the point of his self-esteem, the devil tries to win him for himself. He tries to convince Becker that there is no law governing man, that man is autonomous. But, assisted by Tauler, Becker confronts him with the existence of the conscience as a sign of a higher power to which man is responsible. The fact that his suicide is prevented by a coincidence of factors bordering on the miraculous is another proof that there must be a power stronger than the devil or human despair.

After Becker has reached the nadir, after he has gone through the "Gate of Terror and Despair" (Nov 18, II, 297), he is ready for the acceptance of Christianity and for submission to the will of God: "I submit myself to you, eternal God" (Nov 18, II, 401). Indeed, his long path shows that he tries to completely blot out his own ego, in order to be able to abandon himself fully to God. Tauler seems to demand it of him: "All selfhood (*Ichheit*) must be completely abandoned" (Nov 18, II, 424). That, in spite of unconditional submission to the will of God, man still remains the doer, the guilty, responsible actor, is one of the many paradoxes encountered in Döblin's works.

At this point, Becker's musings have reached a tentative conclusion. He now must put his perceptions into practice in everyday life. Reflection must become action. He returns to his old profession as a high school teacher and, in interpreting *Oedipus* and *Antigone*, deals anew with the very problems that concern him most. *Oedipus* demonstrates for him once again the complete helplessness of man against his inevitable fate: again the question of the possibility of human action and responsibility arises.

Antigone must choose between a human and a divine law. She feels, like Becker, responsible to a divine law but is thereby destroyed. What is discussed in the classroom, in the course of reading *Antigone*, happens to Becker in real life: he follows in the footsteps of Antigone. In trying to straighten out the affair which unfolds around the homosexually inclined school principal, Becker sees once again the limits of the possibilities of the individual who feels bound by a general human law and who proves completely helpless in the face of society's corruption. Becker does not conclude from this that society should be radically changed, but rather that he is still too full of hopes. This event is supposed to make his impotence and weakness even clearer. Becker becomes completely aware of this when, in search of the principal's "friend," Heinz, he stumbles into the battle at the police headquarters, one of the few times that the fate of the revolution and the personal fate of Becker cross. The fact that Becker takes up arms and fights on the side of the revolutionaries has no ideological significance; he wants to be on the side of the suffering and oppressed.[23]

Becker keeps on trying to live his literally understood Christianity, but by so doing he is "catapulted out of the human order" (Nov 18, III, 655) and becomes increasingly isolated. Everything becomes a means of self-experience and self-abandonment. Like other figures created by Döblin, he seeks the purifying power of pain and suffering. He seeks it particularly in self-destruction and thinks that he will be able, in this way, to fulfill Tauler's demand for depersonalization (*"Entichung"*) to the nth degree. But this insane type of self-flagellation is not appropriate, for as Tauler says:

You are to lose your form, to unbind yourself. But in all lostness you should not lose the basis, the life above all life. . . .
You should deny yourself, but in a different way than you are doing now. You should sink deeper and deeper into the unnamed abyss, you should sink where everything loses its name. (Nov 18, III, 642)

In mystic images and metaphors, the union with the primordial basis (*"Urgrund"*) which is no longer the basis of Döblin's philosophy of nature, but of God is postulated. It is typical of Döblin's irrationalism that he has the mystic Tauler speak here, and

"Why Write, and for Whom?"

that mystic ideas and expressions occupy the foreground.

Becker continues on the *via dolorosa*, the way of complete submission, he has chosen, for no single sacrifice but "only the sacrificer" (Nov 18, III, 643) can reach God. The absoluteness of this self-imposed demand stamps him a sectarian and an outsider. But this very attempt to practice a Christianity understood in this absolute form is only another form of pride, so that he finally falls into the hands of the devil. Becker forms a pact with the devil, who wants to show him the nothingness of man and the unconsciousness of human life. The devil adds the soul of a sailor to that of Becker's; the foreign, evil soul seems to win, and Becker becomes a criminal. Again pride has misled him, for he thought that he was equal to the other soul and the devil and felt that he had to suffer for the guilty. He believes too much in himself. Real humility is missing, although—or perhaps because—he tries to practice it externally. As in *Berlin Alexanderplatz*, an apocalyptic battle between the devil and the representative of God ensues. Although because of the fear of the police Becker's body is thrown into the water, Satan is driven off and Becker's soul raised. As in Goethe's *Faust*, Becker's striving is rewarded in the end.

More than the preceding works, *Babylonische Wandrung* and *Amazonas*, the trilogy *November 1918* must be taken as a sign of crisis. The failure of the revolution was a fact whose results Döblin had personally experienced and was still experiencing. Society here appears as corrupt. Even the positive figures, especially Becker's mother, with her affirmation of life and her readiness to help, can change it but little. His tormented search for God drives Becker into complete isolation.[24] What remains seems to be only hope in the grace of God. A gloomy picture indeed! As Friedrich Becker, Döblin, whom one can at least partially identify with his protagonist, had reached the nadir.

[135]

CHAPTER 8

Return to Europe—The Novel Hamlet

THE struggle for God and the retreat into inwardness, as reflected especially in the fate of Becker, dominate this phase of Döblin's work; the personal and confessional statement prevails. "There is a time in the life of everyone when the personal, the most personal, proves to be the most general, the truest and the most real," Döblin wrote to Arnold Zweig.[1] Even the subtitle of the book *Schicksalsreise* ("Journey of Fate"), begun in 1940 and published 1949, namely *Bericht und Bekenntnis* ("Report and Confession") shows this change clearly.

It is also evident in the treatises, mostly written in the USA but published in Germany between 1946 and 1949. In 1943 Döblin wrote *Der Oberst und der Dichter oder das menschliche Herz* ("The Colonel and the Poet or the Human Heart"; published in 1946): a militarist, the glorifier of power and strength, has to defend himself before a judge. Since there is no making an impression on the soldier, the judge changes into a conjurer and poet and presents, in individual episodes, the strengths and weaknesses of the human heart to him. The soldier realizes that goodness and unselfishness, but not wars, have preserved mankind, but he fights this perception and tries to reject it. Just as Konrad in *Babylonische Wandrung* realizes that he contains both good and evil, that he takes part in Georg and Christ, here, too, the human heart includes both. At the end, the panorama is broadened: the archangel Gabriel puts in a good word with God for the despairing poet. But God is angry with men because they do not find the way to Him and do not submit to Him—Becker's theme surfaces again. As long as men do not give up their pride, God will lead them to wars against each other, until they submit in humility. Döblin's basic theme is easily recognizable. The great concern of Expressionism resurfaces in a new fashion: the new man, a vision, which Döblin interprets in his own way. "I affirm

Return to Europe—The Novel Hamlet

the answer which the little book provides, which basically demands the change (and resignation) of man."[2]

If there can be no doubt about Döblin's sincerity, it is nonetheless obvious that the struggle with God was his most personal problem. That he returned to naïve religious images in his attempt to portray the things which concerned him—simply, that God, angels, and devils now appear in his work—is unconvincing because of the naïveté with which it is done. Earlier, his world view and view of man formed a unity with the epic form which he created to express that world view. Now form and content fall completely apart. Nowhere is that clearer than in *Der Oberst und der Dichter*, a poorly disguised didactic piece for which the designation "story" no longer fits. In his attempt to raise his object stylistically, Döblin uses primitive verse that immediately reminds the student of his minstrel-song inserts in *Berlin Alexanderplatz*, but here the verse is completely out of place, since it no longer has a real function.[3] What is said here is valid, *cum grano salis,* also for the other stories, for the parody "Reiseverkehr mit dem Jenseits," the *Märchen vom Materialismus,* and for "Die Pilgerin Aetheria," in which elements of his world view are all too apparent.

The two most important books expressing Döblin's world view at this time are *Unsere Sorge, der Mensch* ("Man, Our Concern") and, above all, the dialogue on religion, *Der unsterbliche Mensch* ("Immortal Man"). Here, in a dialogue between an old man and a young one, Döblin tries to blend his philosophy of nature with the idea of a personal God and to defend his religious convictions against the purely scientific-technical orientation of the young man. The conversation is the most honest and, because of the lack of any literary trappings, the most convincing confrontation of Döblin with himself and Christianity at this time. It represents the sum of all the ideas that moved him, and since here the anonymous, suprapersonal, primeval base is identified with the personal God, the work reaches its zenith in Christian ideas.[4] Despite all the esthetic shortcomings which pervade these writings, and ignoring the question whether Döblin's arguments convince us, his stubborn search for truth deserves our respect. He did not make it easy for himself.

This never ending search for truth is also a characteristic trait of Döblin's last novel, *Hamlet,* subtitled *oder die lange Nacht nimmt ein Ende* ("or the Long Night Comes to an End"). It was published one year before his death and only ten years after its completion. Many critics, probably unjustly, consider it a brilliant work of old age. In any case, it does recapture, to a great degree, the tautness and unity of composition which was only too painfully lacking in the two large trilogies.

The novel was begun in 1945 in Hollywood and finished in Baden-Baden one year later. It is not improbable that Döblin got the idea for the beginning of the novel—the return of a wounded soldier to his parents' house in England—from a novel which he had had to revise in Hollywood.[5]

Like Friedrich Becker, Edward Allison returns wounded from the war and, like him, in his search for truth he also asks how such a war could come about, and who is responsible, using these questions as the point of departure. This questioning does not find its solution in politico-social circumstances; the appeal to humaneness is—as has repeatedly been shown—characteristic of the late Döblin. His old theme surfaces once more in the form of the question of whether man is a free responsible agent or a marionette ruled by anonymous powers. This is constantly discussed in the novel, whose title already indicates that Shakespeare's *Hamlet* serves as a model for the situation of the hero, Edward Allison. For, like Hamlet, Edward Allison, upon his return, finds guilt and deception in his parent's home. The fate of the two protagonists is similar, for both return home, look for the truth of human relationships in their homes, and are constantly caught in a web of truth and lies, reality and illusion. But their fates are also different, for Hamlet is destroyed, but Edward overcomes the "Hamlet ghost" (Ha, 573) and regains at least the hope of a meaningful life.

Döblin typically approaches the question of the possibility of responsible action and of the essence of human existence. In the house of Edward's father, the writer Gordon Allison, stories are told to entertain the wounded son. These stories, frequently parodies of stories from world literature, correspond exactly to Döblin's ideas concerning the novella-like independence of individual parts of a novel. They have a double function. First of all, they illustrate definite views of man. Rather than doing so abstractly, the figures discuss philosophical problems with the help of illustrations in which two views of man are diametrically op-

Return to Europe—The Novel Hamlet

posed: either man is the product of supraindividual powers which move him and act in his stead, or he is independent and thus completely responsible for his actions. Secondly—and increasingly so—the function of the stories consists in gradually unveiling the true identity of Edward's parents, and revealing the true beings behind the illusion of their masks. What is thus revealed is likewise a well-known motif in Döblin's works, that of the battle of the sexes, which—as already demonstrated—is grounded in autobiographical experiences.[6] Because the stories are open to diverse interpretations, a very complex net of relationships arises.

After Gordon Allison has initially been described as a man "with an interchangeable personality" (Ha, 42), he begins the cycle of tales with "Die Prinzessin von Tripoli" ("The Princess of Tripoli"), a tale from the age of the Crusades told by Swinburne, among others. This story is stripped of illusion and treated ironically by Allison. He peels off its romantic layer by placing the figure of the minnesinger Jaufie in the cultural and social conditions of his own age. He wants to show that man is not a free agent, but rather a product of custom, society, and world view, that is, he is controlled by suprapersonal powers. Thus he comes to the conclusion:

You think you're in the saddle, you seem to be riding; later it seems to be different to you. Sometimes you get the impression: there is a spider and a web. We are not the spider, but the fly that struggles in the web. (Ha, 49)

Edward is not satisfied with this answer. Just as his father had clarified his position in a story, he clarifies his in a fable. The lion on the mountain, Mondora, sees his own reflection in a lake, does not recognize himself, and drowns attempting to fight it. In his relentless search for truth, Edward not only identifies himself with the seeker Kierkegaard but is also like the lion. He no longer recognizes his own reflection. A harmonic image of man has not only been externally destroyed by the war and the amputation of his leg, but, much worse, the essential image of man has become unrecognizable to him. He desperately seeks his identity—in self-analysis and through tearing the masks from others. By exposing their existences as roles, he is thus able to get at their real beings. But the fable poses anew the central question of the novel: does man only see a fantom when he beholds his mirror image?

Edward is not alone in his attempt to refute his father. The legend of the page and the ring, told by Miss Virginia, is supposed to demonstrate that man is not the product of supraindividual powers, but that, on the contrary, the powers originate from a new man. In spite of this, Gordon Allison sticks to his position. He does not believe in the possibility of individual freedom. In his opinion men are marionettes dangling on invisible strings; they do not exist as responsible individuals.

Even in his conversations with James Mackenzie, his maternal uncle, Edward does not find satisfactory answers to his questions. Mackenzie is an intelligent, unmarried professor concerned with obscure subjects, an admirer of Indian wisdom who observes the tension-filled Allison house from a distance. The theses which he proposes are undoubtly taken from Döblin's philosophy of nature: a truly human existence is only possible through self-abandonment and conscious participation in the supraindividual process of nature. Only by self-abandonment can one achieve a perception of the true relationships, "a flowing together of one with another. From the duality of ego and world, a non-duality arises" (Ha, 203). The discussion of *Wadzek* and *Babylonische Wandrung* has shown that Döblin liked to be ironic and skeptical about his own position. The same is true of *Hamlet*. What is proposed by "the pensive professor who knew everything and yet avoided himself and everything else" (Ha, 399) is put in an ironic light by the manner in which he is described. Edward brusquely rejects his ideas in which he sees only a deceptive maneuver designed to distract him from his relentless questioning.

The stories are intended not only to illustrate opposite points of view, but also to reveal the true identity of Gordon and Alice Allison; and this function moves more and more clearly into the foreground. This is especially true of the story of King Lear which is related by Mackenzie. In a manner typical of the novel, the figure of Lear is demythologized in the narration; indeed, Lear himself battles against his enslavement by the myth. Mackenzie depicts him as a cunning ruler who, with a boundless vitality, would like to eliminate all limits. But in this story the professor is not merely trying to characterize his brother-in-law.

Return to Europe—The Novel Hamlet

The story also contains a negative example of his thesis by showing the insatiable ego that does not want to submit: "It wants to correspond to nothing. It wants to be unique, unmistakable. It wants no relationships. 'I' can only count up to one. No harmony arises." (Ha, 280) While Gordon Allison sees himself reconfirmed—there is no reality as we imagine it, but what we call reality is always dominated by images and fantasies formed independently of the will of the individual—for Edward it seems that Lear's destruction reinforces the responsibility of man.

Edward seeks the causes of the war from which he himself has suffered and will suffer for the rest of his life. Ever more clearly he thinks that the reasons for the catastrophe lie in the nature of man. He concentrates more and more on the fate of his parents. Edward lives the Hamlet figure; thus there is no need to retell the story of the Danish prince. The parallels between Edward and his literary model become progressively closer. The veteran tries to learn the history of his parents, which is told him partly indirectly and partly directly. Alice, who had vied for his love and affection with two stories of mothers awaiting the homecoming of their sons, represents herself as the sinner Salome and as St. Theodora, as the dancer who drunkenly abandons herself to the Dionysian frenzy of life and as the penitent who withdraws from life—a familiar polarity in Döblin's works. In the myth of Pluto and Proserpina, she portrays her view of the tragic fate of her marriage to Gordon. The latter answers with an interpretation of Michelangelo's sonnets in whose gloomy melancholy he sees himself reflected—his longing for love, and his inability to love.

Edward's penetrating search for the truth altogether destroys the apparent harmony in the Allison house. The terrible love-hate relationship of the parents comes out into the open. The ground is taken out from under the roles they had played up to now, and the whole abyss of human passions behind their apparently peaceful life opens up. After Edward has become an unwilling witness of a terrible scene between his parents, Gordon and, later, his daughter, Kathleen, leave home. Alice, who tried to draw her son over to her side and to make him an instrument of revenge on her hated spouse, seems to triumph. However, when she completely reveals Gordon's history and his relation to London's underworld to Edward, and even lies to him about a former lover and about Gordon not being his real father—which she does only to get her son completely on her side—a break also occurs between them. "The long night of lies is past" (Ha, 420). By his quest, Hamlet-Edward has uncovered not only the true character of his parent's marriage, but sees himself once more confronted by the experience that dark instincts beyond human reason and will seem to determine the fate of man.

Alice also leaves home. She declares herself completly free and unfettered, but it is freedom from everything, not freedom to do something. Because there is no longer a center of values for her by which she can orient herself it does not matter what she does. Her supposed path to absolute freedom is, in reality, the path to emptiness and anxiety. However, it is also the path to total self-abandonment. Thus in the final part when she becomes a medium in the clairvoyant act of a questionable artist, she has reached the nadir.

On the other side, Gordon has, by the very dissolution of his marriage, learned that it was not blind chance that brought him and Alice together, but a profound necessity, for only reciprocally can they save each other. For him, there is no "I" without a "Thou." Gordon thus abandons the point of view he had assumed in his narrations. He begins to look for his wife, but when he has found her, he is mortally wounded by the artist. For the first time, however, both spouses confront each other as human beings, and Gordon dies reconciled with his wife and with himself. Alice follows him a little later in death, she, too, reconciled with her life, after she has understood the path to "freedom" as a form of expiation. Edward, too, undergoes a similar positive development: he discovers life as a task and a great relationship. He retracts the play in which he had tried to expose the chameleon-like changeability in the character of his father and, at the same time, to expose life as a meaningless cycle in the peculiar ambiguity of these parts of the novel. As with Hamlet, the search for the truth in human relationships does not end in death, but with an optimistic view of life, which he begins to rediscover and in which he sees a task that is, not by chance, of a social and charitable nature. As always with Döblin, here, too, we have an open ending which does not completely satisfy us, because Edward has little basis for the optimism he shows after his experience. Thus we are confronted with a dialectic leap,

Return to Europe—The Novel Hamlet

something not at all unique in Döblin's works. In an earlier version of the novel, he enters a monastery to avoid life, while confronting it in the published version. These two different endings reveal, once again, the polarity of activity and passivity which permeates Döblin and his entire work.[7]

CHAPTER 9

Conclusion

THE favorable bias with which the author views this monograph must not be allowed to lead to an overestimation of Döblin's works. Döblin surely stands in the shadow of the great novelists of the first half of this century: Thomas Mann, Hermann Broch, and Robert Musil. The lack of translations of other important works besides *Berlin Alexanderplatz* is, as it were, the most cogent proof of this fact.

A comparison with the works of the novelists mentioned above shows at once their difference from Döblin and the specific quality of his "Döblinism." While his theory of the novel hardly sets doctrinaire limits to the form of the novel (he actually defines it as the completely free form), in his own works he prefers a language of form (*Formensprache*) which is clearly differentiated from that of the other writers. Like many of his great contemporaries, he polemicizes against psychology, causality, and erotic themes, against one-dimensional and linear plots.[1] And he aims—in his unmistakable manner—at totality and complexity. Since the dynamics of the actions in which the individual is imbedded is most important for him, he foregoes reflective excursions and thus renounces the characteristic of the polyhistorical novel, as it occurs in Otto Flake, Broch, and Musil. Döblin wanted to be an epic writer in the original sense, rather than a novelist. He simply wanted to tell a story, not to philosophize. The proliferating narrative mood, the formlessness of many of his works, the frequently noted weaknesses of his novels' endings are only the consequences of an epic attitude which views the epic as endless and thus picks up the thread broken off in one novel in the next. Just as he always judged lyric poetry negatively, as the most esoteric of all literary forms, Döblin mistrusted a theory of the novel which, in his opinion, nearly weighed down with "culture" and knowledge, exceeded by far what he took to

Conclusion

be the purpose of the epic: the representation of the great basic human motion in the framework of an overpowering and pervasive relationship with life and nature. The consolatory feeling of being included in this natural relationship, a basic cosmic feeling, binds him closely to the many Expressionists whom he otherwise viewed with reserve. It also contains an irrationalism pointing toward mysticism, thus creating an opposition to the intellectuality of the polyhistorical novel which, in his eyes, must per force obviate the democratization of art which he desired. Just because he consciously tried to open literature not only to the so-called educated bourgeoisie, but to all classes, he must have regretted the absence of a stronger echo.

Success came with *Berlin Alexanderplatz*, a work that, by no coincidence, relies on underworld motifs to a much greater degree than all his other works. Although religious themes were by no means overlooked, these motifs have contributed greatly to the popularity of the book, whose success has unfortunately overshadowed Döblin's other epic works. Nonetheless, it was *Die Geschichte vom Franz Biberkopf* which established the renown of its author and assured him a place in the history of world literature. Given these limitations, and with the additional limitation that only a few of his works written after 1933 have found, or will find, general favor, Döblin may be regarded as one of the great German prose writers of the first third of this century. Like hardly any other writer, he portrayed the impotence and abandonment of man, but at the same time made a postulate from this insight by describing the necessity of submission to the relationships of life and nature, to the great mass beings, while claiming that sacrifice is unavoidable. But in a dialectic turnabout, the rebellion and protest of the individual which, for its part, can lead to the (technological) hubris of man results from the insight into the impotence and the necessity of submission; and subsequently it causes another turnabout. This is an endless process, one of the essential modes of human existence which Döblin—in accordance with his concept of the epic writer—wanted to bring to light.

Thus Döblin stands in the middle of the traditional concept of a free and great personality which achieves its final peak in Nietzsche's concept of the Superman, and the total dismantling of the personality to a mere object of anonymous powers, as so frequently happens in the present. The "dialectical tension" between the two extremes is not eased in Döblin's work but continuously results in turnabouts. To have portrayed this dialectic movement in moving images is Döblin's great accomplishment.

Notes and References

Chapter One

1. "Autobiographische Skizze," Zl, 56–57. In a letter to his friends Elvira and Arthur Rosin, dated January 22, 1950, Döblin wrote: "Thank you very much for your friendly and thoughtful remarks on my book *Schicksalsreise* which I wrote only incidentally. I am not a man of autobiography, and I prefer to fix my eyes solely on the external world and on other people" (Br. 405).
2. *Doktor Döblin. Selbstbiographie*, ed. Heinz Graber (Berlin, 1970).
3. AD. I'm Buch. . . .
4. Letter to Hermann Kesten dated July 24, 1941, Br, 255.
5. "Erster Rückblick," Zl, 131.
6. *Ibid.*, p. 141.
7. *Ibid*. The play was *Lydia und Mäxchen. Tiefe Verbeugung in einem Akt*, and the pseudonym Alfred Börne.
8. *Ibid.*, p. 142.
9. "Grosstadt und Grosstädter," Zl, 138.
10. Leo Kreutzer, *Alfred Döblin. Sein Werk bis 1933* (Stuttgart, 1970), pp. 20–21. Minder's disciple, Louis Huguet, in his extensive and unusually careful interpretation of Döblin's works, also begins with the family tragedy and other autobiographical material by successfully applying the categories and views of psychoanalysis (Freud, Jung, Krafft-Ebing, Otto Rank) and thereby gaining entirely new perspectives. (The work is unfortunately still unpublished.)
11. "Epilog," Al, 385.
12. Besides the work of Louis Huguet already mentioned, see the article by Robert Minder, "Die Segelfahrt von Alfred Döblin. Struktur und Erlebnis. Mit unbekanntem biographischem Material," *Gestaltungsgeschichte und Gesellschaftsgeschichte. Literatur-, Kunst- und Musikwissenschaftliche Studien* ed. Helmut Kreutzer in collaboration with Käte Hamburger (Stuttgart, 1969), pp. 461–486.
13. *Ibid.*
14. "Autobiographische Skizze," Zl, 57. See also: "Arzt und Dichter," Al, 363.

15. *Die Neue Rundschau,* XXV (1914), 1717–1722.
16. "Es ist Zeit," *Die Neue Rundschau,* XXVIII (1917), 1011.
17. *Ibid.,* p. 1012.
18. *Ibid.,* p. 1011.
19. *Ibid.,* p. 1014.
20. "Drei Demokratien," *Die Neue Rundschau,* XXIX (1918), 254–262.
21. "Revolutionstage im Elsas's," *Die Neue Rundschau,* XXX (1919), 621–632.
22. Letter dated December 15, 1918, Br, 104.
23. Letter dated December 23, 1918, Br, 105.
24. "Dämmerung," *Die Neue Rundschau,* XXX (1919), 1281.
25. *Ibid.,* p. 1287.
26. *Ibid.*
27. "Republik," *Die Neue Rundschau,* XXXI (1920), 75.
28. *Ibid.,* p. 77.
29. *Ibid.,* p. 79.
30. Letter to Wilhelm Lehmann dated September 1, 1923, Br, 123.
31. *Reise in Polen* (Berlin, 1925), reprinted in *Ausgewählte Werke in Einzelbänden* (Freiburg i. Br., 1968); here quoted from the latter edition.
32. See Martin Esslin, *Brecht. Das Paradox des politischen Dichters* (Frankfurt/Main, Bonn, 1962), p. 50.
33. *Ibid.,* p. 53.
34. On the occasion of his enrollment, Döblin had to fill out a personal data sheet; in the short biography attached to it he reinforced his unusual attitude toward art: "I do not want to forget: I come from Jewish parents. And secondly: I have never viewed my literary works as works of art in the contemporary, specialized sense and written them accordingly, but rather as intellectual works serving that life which is of an intellectual type" (Br, 140).
35. Letter dated March 3, 1928, Br, 140 f.
36. *Das Tagebuch,* XI (May, 1930), 696–698.
37. At this point, I am following Kreutzer's presentation, *Alfred Döblin,* pp. 134–147.
38. *Literatur und Dichtung im Dritten Reich.* Eine Dokumentation von Josef Wulf (Reinbek bei Hamburg, 1966), pp. 16–19.
39. Letter dated March 4, 1933, Br, 172.
40. Letter dated December 16, 1934, Br, 199.
41. The film was supposed to bear the title "Die geweihten Töchter" ("The Consecrated Daughters"). The following remarks in a letter to Efraim Frisch from 1921 show how much Döblin learned from movies and how closely his concept agrees with his theory of the novel and with the technique of *Berlin Alexanderplatz:* "Can you do anything with my film? Read it carefully: I'll stand up for it. It contains

Notes and References

three innovations: 1) the abandonment of the field of tension (*"Spannungsfeld"*) in favor of groups of scenes mediated by "transformations," so that an amalgamation of elements according to their meaning is achieved; 2) imaginary space beside naturalistic space, a device of greatest importance for the author and for the spiritualization of the whole thing; 3) completely optical fantasizing, a minimum of words (two sentences and two titles)" (Br, 117).

42. "A writer carries a piece of his homeland in him with his language, and an amputation (the change to another language) is fatal," Döblin wrote on February 9, 1944 to Elvira and Arthur Rosin (Br, 300).

43. See Anthony W. Riley, "The Professing Christian and the Ironic Humanist: A Comment on the Relationship of Alfred Döblin and Thomas Mann after 1933," *Essays on German Literature in Honour of G. Joyce Hallamore*, eds. Michael S. Batts and Marketa S. Stankiewicz (Toronto, 1968), pp. 177–194. See also Paul Rilla, "Literatur und Lüth. Eine Streitschrift," *Deutsche Literaturkritik der Gegenwart*, vol. IV, 1, ed. Hans Mayer (Stuttgart, 1971), pp. 320–401.

44. Letter to Arthur Rosin dated June 30, 1945, Br, 318. In a letter to Arthur Rosin dated June 12, 1944, Döblin stated with similar resignation: "In fact, not a single line of mine has been published since I've been here; for better or worse, I must realize that I am completely out of place here" (Br, 304).

45. The title refers to the Golden Gate Bridge in San Francisco, where the first large international peace conference took place in 1945.

Chapter Two

1. "Autobiographische Skizze," Zl, 56.
2. Letter dated November 10, 1904, Br, 26.
3. *Ibid.*
4. "Stille Bewohner des Rollschranks," Zl, 117 f. On this novel and the earlier works in general see especially Ernst Ribbat, *Die Wahrheit des Lebens im frühen Werk Alfred Döblins* (Münster, 1970) (Münstersche Beiträge zur deutschen Literaturwissenschaft 4).
5. Letter to the publisher, Axel Juncker, dated April 9, 1904, Br, 23. See also the letter to Fritz Mauthner dated October 24, 1903, Br, 21.
6. See Horst Denkler, *Drama des Expressionismus, Programm–Spieltext–Theater* (Munich, 1967), especially pp. 38–42.
7. Now reprinted in *Einakter und kleine Dramen des Expressionismus*, ed. Horst Denkler (Stuttgart, 1968), pp. 22–46.
8. "Epilog," Al, 385 f.
9. See especially the *Märchen vom Materialismus* (Stuttgart, 1959), written in 1943 in Hollywood.
10. Letter to Herwarth Walden dated November 22, 1905, Br, 32 f.

11. *Einakter und kleine Dramen des Expressionismus*, p. 45.
12. "Autobiographische Skizze," Zl, 57.
13. See Ribbat, *Die Wahrheit des Lebens im frühen Werk Alfred Döblins.*
14. In his little-known dissertation, "Döblin's Godless Mysticism" (Princeton, 1965), Robert Bruce Kimber has properly interpreted these novellas by applying to them the ideas pertaining to Döblin's philosophy of nature. To be sure, Döblin's two philosophical works appeared in 1927 (*Das Ich über der Natur*) and 1933 (*Unser Dasein*), but the nucleus of his ideas was developed about 1905—according to Döblin's own statement. In the early 1920's, Döblin began to present his ideas in a series of articles published in various magazines.
15. *Der deutsche Maskenball* (Berlin, 1921), p. 36.
16. *Ibid.*, p. 80.

Chapter Three

1. See the articles by Manfred Durzak, "Flake und Döblin. Ein Kapitel in der Geschichte des polyhistorischen Romans," *Germanisch-Romanische Monatsschrift*, XX (1970), 286–305; by Wolfgang Grothe, "Die Theorie des Erzählens bei Alfred Döblin," *Text und Kritik*, 13/14 (June, 1966), 5–21; and by Viktor Zmegač, "Alfred Döblins Poetik des Romans," *Sinn und Form*, XXI (1969), 404–423.
2. Especially in the essay "Nutzen der Musik für die Literatur," Zl, 158–160.
3. Gottfried Benn, "Probleme der Lyrik," Benn, *Essays, Reden, Vorträge*, ed. Dieter Wellershoff (Wiesbaden, 2nd ed., 1962), p. 498.
4. Armin Arnold, "Der neue Mensch als Gigant. Döblins frühe Romane," Arnold, *Die Literatur des Expressionismus. Sprachliche und thematische Quellen* (Stuttgart, 1966), pp. 80–107.
5. "An Romanautoren und ihre Kritiker. Berliner Programm," Al, 18.
6. *Ibid.*, p. 16.
7. *Ibid.*, p. 18 f.
8. *Ibid.*, p. 16.
9. *Ibid.*, p. 19.
10. "Der Bau des epischen Werks," Al, 107.
11. Letter to Albert Ehrenstein from 1919 (?), Br, 109.
12. "Schriftstellerei und Dichtung," Al, 91 f.
13. *Ibid.*, p. 91.
14. *Ibid.*, p. 96.
15. "Bemerkungen zum Roman," Al, 21.
16. "An Romanautoren und ihre Kritiker. Berliner Programm," Al, 17.
17. "Der Bau des epischen Werks," Al, 113.

Notes and References

18. "An Romanautoren und ihre Kritiker. Berliner Programm," Al, 18.
19. "Der Bau des epischen Werks," Al, 106.
20. "Staat und Schriftsteller," Al, 57.
21. "Der historische Roman und wir," Al, 178.
22. "Staat und Schriftsteller," Al, 57.
23. *Ibid.*
24. "Impressionen von einer Rheinreise," Zl, 173.
25. On the religious development of Alfred Döblin see Monique Weyembergh-Boussart, *Alfred Döblin, Seine Religiosität in Persönlichkeit und Werk* (Bonn, 1970) (Abhandlungen zur Kunst-, Musik- und Literaturwissenschaft 76).
26. *Die Erhebung. Jahrbuch für neu Dichtung und Wertung*, ed. Alfred Wolfenstein I (Berlin, 1919), pp. 381–398.
27. See Robert Bruce Kimber, "Döblin's Godless Mysticism" (Princeton, 1965).
28. AD. Im Buch . . . , 109.

Chapter Four

1. See the letter to Martin Buber dated October 13, 1912, Br, 58 f. Buber was a reader for the publishers Rütten und Loening in Frankfurt am Main and apparently helped Döblin with advice and criticism (letter of October 12, 1915, Br, 76 f.). In the first letter, Döblin notes that he has read everything obtainable, but asks Buber for further references. Among other things, he wrote: "Histories of customs, things of daily life, prose especially from the eighteenth century (Kienlung period): I cannot get enough of these things. Do you know of a decent biography of Kienlung himself? I am dealing with the fate of the Wu-wei sects (under Wang-lun's leadership); do you know of monographs on these or related sects?" Br, 58 f.
2. *The Living Thoughts of Confucius.* Presented by Alfred Döblin (Toronto/New York, 1940).
3. *Der deutsche Maskenball* (Berlin, 1921), p. 105. In regard to sources and quotations from primary and secondary literature, see especially the Afterword to the new edition by Walter Muschg, and Ingrid Schuster's article, "Alfred Döblins Chinesischer Roman," *Wirkendes Wort*, XX (1970), 339–346.
4. "Epilog," Al, 387.
5. "We must stop so much doing and working, stop increasing matter in the world." (IüN, 236 f.)
6. See Döblin's introduction to *The Living Thoughts of Confucius*, where he emphasizes the point that human action should be in harmony with the course of the world, that only man can disrupt the harmony of the cosmos, and that therefore it is his duty to preserve it.

7. "Epilog," Al, 389.

8. In his famous Akademie-Rede, "Der Bau des epischen Werks" (first published in 1929), Döblin stated: "But the epic theme was: one fights in vain and is powerless against power, a weak hero, the Truly Weak One" (Al, 126 f.).

9. The first chapter of the novel, later omitted, shows that the antithesis of rebellion and submission, which dominates the novel, was related less to a general attitude toward life than to a definite politicosocial situation. (Printed under the title "Der Überfall auf Chao-laosu" as an independent story in *Genius. Bilder und Aufsätze zu alter und neuer Kunst,* ed. Carl Georg Heise and Hans Mardersteig (Munich, 1921), pp. 275–285. See also Kreutzer, *Alfred Döblin,* pp. 46–54.)

10. "I admit that, even today, the communication of facts and documents makes me happy, but facts and documents, do you know why? The great epic writer, nature, speaks to me, and I, the small one, stand in front of it and enjoy what my big brother can do. And sometimes it happened to me, when I was writing this or that book, that I could hardly contain myself from simply copying down entire documents and said to myself: I can't do this any better." "Der Bau des epischen Werks" (Al, 113 f.). But Döblin added that the author, too, had to enter into the objectivity which he had so long revered.

11. Roland Links, *Alfred Döblin* (Berlin, 1965), pp. 46–49 and Hansjörg Elshorst, *Mensch und Umwelt im Werk Alfred Döblins* (Diss. Munich, 1966), p. 27. On October 12, 1915, Döblin wrote to Martin Buber: the book "became quite different from what I had planned (I planned to describe the technology of gigantic Berlin, but it became something very human, the first part of it, a book about how technology expels someone, a comic book, of course vacillating between the painfully comic, the humanly serious, and the purely comic . . .)" (Br, 77).

12. The suspicion arises here that Döblin wanted to treat the "O-Mensch-Pathos" of the Expressionists ironically.

13. See Erich Fromm, *Escape from Freedom* (New York, 1968).

14. Al, 387.

15. See the letter to Martin Buber dated December 13, 1915: "Didn't you see this weakling, this Don Quixote, 'Wadzek', as he struggles against his fate with his companion 'Schneemann', brings his weakness to a climactic catastrophe,—how, broken, he travels several routes unconsciously, and then in a half dream, lost and sold out, swims to America? The lovingly comic feeling opposite the seemingly tragic appears and vents itself in so many places in the book" (Br, 80).

Notes and References

Chapter Five

1. "Autobiographische Skizze," Al, 57.
2. Günter Grass, Über meinen Lehrer Döblin," *Akzente*, XIV (1967), 304.
3. "Epilog," Al, 387 f.
4. Al, 163–186.
5. *Ibid.*, p. 173.
6. *Ibid.*
7. *Ibid.*, p. 181.
8. *Ibid.*, p. 182.
9. *Der deutsche Maskenball*, p. 127.
10. In a letter to Herwarth Walden dated December 10, 1916, Döblin remarked that the actual war would soon be at an end, but that, in domestic politics, war was on the point of starting, a war which would draw the consequences of the foreign war. "Watchword: Germany against East Prussia, Europe against feudalism; hopefully then politics will get us unpolitical people involved. Stupidity: the party à la Hiller, etc.; every party has the intelligence it needs, I am against speculators, Social Democrats, Agrarians, Literarians, but the remnants of feudalism in the army, in bureaucracy must be done away with—also they must be pushed back beyond the Njemen and Düna rivers" (Br, 87). See Leo Kreutzer, *Alfred Döblin*, pp. 55–70; and Günter Grass's essay, note 2 above.
11. "Der Epiker, sein Stoff und die Kritik," Al, 339 f.
12. *Der deutsche Maskenball*, p. 128.
13. See the "Dedication" in *Berge Meere und Giganten*, where the irrational power of life is conjured up as follows: "Trembling, grasping, vibrating centipede, thousand-spirit, thousand-header."
14. See "Der Epiker, sein Stoff und die Kritik," Al, 343 f.
15. "Bemerkungen zu *Berge Meere und Giganten*," Al, 345.
16. "Lusitania. Drei Szenen," *Die Gefährten*, III (1920), 1–59.
17. *Die Nonnen von Kemnade. Schauspiel in vier Akten* (Berlin, 1923). See "Einleitung," p. 9 f.
18. *Ibid.*, p. 80.
19. *Der deutsche Maskenball*, p. 53.
20. Al, 62–83. The essay first appeared in 1924, at the time of the publication of the novel in *Die Neue Rundschau*.
21. *Ibid.*, p. 64.
22. *Ibid.*, p. 74.
23. *Ibid.*, p. 83.
24. Letter to Efraim Frisch dated February 11, 1921, Br, 120.
25. "Epilog," Al, 388.
26. *Ibid.*

27. "Bemerkungen zu *Berge Meere und Giganten,*" Al, 350.
28. *Ibid.,* p. 351.
29. *Ibid.*
30. *Ibid.,* p. 352.
31. *Ibid.,* p. 353.
32. *Ibid.*
33. *Ibid.,* p. 354.
34. Robert Minder, "Alfred Döblin," *Deutsche Literatur des XX. Jahrhunderts,* eds. H. Friedmann und Otto Mann, vol. II (Heidelberg, 1961), p. 150.
35. Al, 389.
36. "Nachwort zu *Giganten,*" Al, 373.
37. *Ibid.*
38. *Ibid.,* p. 374.

Chapter Six

1. Al, 389. Döblin is speaking of the book *Berge Meere und Giganten* (1924).
2. *Ibid.* One very important source is Helmut von Glasenapp's book on Hinduism (Munich, 1922). Among the travelogues which Döblin mentions only in passing are: Emil Schlagintweit, *Indien in Wort und Bild,* 2 vols. (Leipzig, 1880, 1881), and Ludwig Halla, *Untere Palmen und in Märchentempeln* (Berlin, 1914). The major motif of the poem, the conquest of death by love (Sawitri), stems from an episode reported in the *Mahabharata.* But it must be emphasized that Döblin—in accord with his principle of factual imagination—deals very freely with the material selected on the basis of an inner affinity. The origin of the name of the main figure, Manas, for instance is not completely clear. In Sanskrit it symbolizes the organ of thought, but no person. It is possible that Döblin used the abstract name of the organ as the basis for the observation of the self and the world by his figure. See Heinz Graber, *Alfred Döblins Epos Manas* (Bern, 1967), especially pp. 102–109, the most important study of the work and one of the best on Döblin in general.
3. *Die Erhebung. Jahrbuch für neue Dichtung und Wertung,* ed. Albert Wolfenstein, I (Berlin, 1919), pp. 381–398.
4. "Buddho und die Natur," *Die Neue Rundschau,* XXXII (1921), 1194.
5. *Ibid.,* p. 1200.
6. In the essay "Bemerkungen zu *Berge Meere und Giganten,*" Döblin says that he could not resist the purely linguistic impulse and continues: "The high level of many passages, their solemn, hymnal character contribute to this. I also want to confess that I no longer had the feeling of being in the realm of real, ordinary prose, in language.

Notes and References

Where the journey will lead to I don't know. Old verse forms seem impossible to me. One shouldn't force things, shouldn't try too, hard, and should let everything happen by itself" (Al, 355).

7. "Epilog," Al, 389.
8. Heinz Graber has rightly stressed the meaning of the return motif in Döblin's works; see Graber, *Alfred Döblins Epos Manas*, p. 66 f.
9. Robert Musil, "Alfred Döblins Epos," *Manas*, pp. 375–381; also in Musil, *Prosa, Dramen, späte Briefe*, ed. Adolf Frisé (Hamburg, 1957), pp. 613–619.
10. Döblin's fiftieth birthday also fell in the year 1928. On this occasion, the book *Alfred Döblin. Im Buch. Zu Haus. Auf der Strasse*, presented by Alfred Döblin and Oskar Loerke was published. It contains—besides important autobiographical essays by Döblin—an excellent introductory essay by his friend and colleague in the Academy, Oskar Loerke, entitled "Das bisherige Werk Alfred Döblins" ("Alfred Döblin's Works to Date"). Even now, this essay belongs to the best that has been written about Döblin. Like Ferdinand Lion in a similar article, Loerke puts Döblin's philosophy of nature at the center of his discussion, a fact which Döblin gratefully acknowledged. (See his letter to Ferdinand Lion dated March 3, 1928, Br, 140 f.)
11. Wolfgang Peitz, *Alfred Döblin Bibliographie 1905–1966* (Freiburg i. Br., 1968), pp. 8–9, 12 (Materialien zur deutschen Literatur I).
12. *Ibid.*, pp. 12–14.
13. Theodore Ziolkowski, *Dimensions of the Modern Novel. German Texts and European Contexts* (Princeton, 1969), p. 129 f.
14. Joris Duytschaever, "Eine Hebbelsatire in Döblins Alexanderplatz," *Etudes Germaniques*, XXIV (1969), 536–552.
15. In *Der deutsche Maskenball*, Döblin gave the description of such a collage (p. 70 f.).
16. See Jürgen Stenzel, "Mit Kleister und Schere. Zur Handschrift von *Berlin Alexanderplatz*," *Text und Kritik*, 13/14 (1966), 41–44.
17. *Unser Dasein*, p. 173.
18. In the fragmentary autobiography *Doktor Döblin*, the author told of the lasting impression which one "Moritat" had made on him: "He roamed the streets alone a lot; once he came upon a fair. On one booth a minstrel story was painted; harshly painted canvas, a terrible murder scene. The boy ran home confused. He could not forget the image; it caused him much anxiety; and many years later the terrible impression, whose pain he had tried to flee, had still not left him." (*Doktor Döblin*, p. VI.)
19. "Epilog," Al, 391. See also the letter to Julius Petersen (September 18, 1931, Br, 165). On October 9, 1947, Döblin wrote to Paul Lüth: "It is as plain as the nose on your face that I have not the least

to do with Joyce, neither in content nor in ideas. As far as the formal aspect goes,—why is it necessary to link me with Joyce? My *Wallenstein* (1918) already had the scene arrangement and the overlapping which evolved at this time and found artistic expression in another area, in film montage. Interior monologue is an old literary device. It was used a thousand times in literature as a monologue, or an aside of the author, as a presentation by the "I" or the "he", and look particularly at Otto Ludwig's "Zwischen Himmel und Erde," the story which unquestionably represents the highest narrative accomplishment I know of in German literature. But the tales of Heinrich von Kleist, masterful and political in their own way, are dramatized stories, show theatrical influences, and lack the specific epic character. Even in *Alexanderplatz* the technique of association plays a great role, and I know it better than Joyce, namely from the living object, from psychoanalysis" (Br, 376 f.).

20. "Epilog," Al, 391.
21. Letter to Julius Petersen dated September 18, 1931, Br. 165 f.
22. Critics have repeatedly attempted to interpret *Berlin Alexanderplatz* in a more concrete sense as a political book. Ziolkowski sees in Franz Biberkopf the German Michel who is fascinated by Hitler (Reinhold) (*Dimensions of the Modern Novel*, p. 126). James H. Reid discerns in Franz Biberkopf an allegory of the fate of Germany between the world wars. Ingenious as they may be, both observations lack a real basis inside or outside the novel. On the other hand, I concur with Reid that the question of solidarity, especially as it is handled in the conversation between Franz and the anarchist (quoted earlier), is essential for the politico-social aspect of the novel. (James H. Reid, "*Berlin Alexanderplatz*—A Political Novel," *German Life and Letters*, XXI (1967/1968), 214–223.)

Chapter Seven

1. Letter to Ferdinand Lion dated April 18, 1933, Br, 179.
2. A different, and more positive, view of one of Döblin's exile novels is taken by Heinz Dieter Osterle in his article: "Alfred Döblins Revolutionstrilogie *November 1918*," *Monatshefte*, LXXII (1970), 9–23.
3. "Epilog," Al, 392.
4. Letter to Heinz Gollong dated January 2, 1934, Br, 184.
5. Letter dated March 22, 1933, Br. 177.
6. Letter to Elvira and Arthur Rosin dated February 23, 1934, Br, 191.
7. "Epilog," Al, 392.
8. See the letter to Herwarth Walden from January, 1904, Br, 121 and footnote 504 f.

Notes and References

9. Specific aspects of Kierkegaard's philosophy seem to have attracted him less than Kierkegaard's penetrating search for truth. Thus Edward Allison can base his own relentless search for truth on the Danish philosopher. (See "Epilog," Al, 394.)

10. "Epilog," Al, 393.

11. Walter Muschg, in attempting to restore the work to its original form, omitted the last part of the novel from his new edition which appeared under the title *Amazonas*. This omission has been justly criticized by Döblin scholars. Here the first two parts are quoted from Muschg's new edition (*Amazonas*), the third part (*Der neue Urwald*) from the 1948 edition.

12. *Der deutsche Maskenball*, pp. 107–109.

13. "Epilog," Al, 393. It is not impossible that Döblin, who often considered his novels as testing grounds for new ideas, also wanted to "test" his idea of a Jewish state that was to be newly founded.

14. Letter to Viktor Zuckerkandl dated October 30, 1936, Br, 214 f.

15. "Epilog," Al, 394.

16. See his essay "Prometheus und das Primitive," *Mass und Wert*, III (1938), 331–351.

17. The first volume of the novel was published in 1939 under the title *Eine deutsche Revolution. Erzählwerk in drei Bänden. Band I: Bürger und Soldaten 1918* (Stockholm, and Amsterdam, 1939). A second part appeared in 1946: *Sieger und Besiegte. Eine wahre Geschichte* (New York, 1946). The entire work finally appeared between 1948 and 1950 in three volumes in Munich. Volume I: *Verratenes Volk;* volume II: *Heimkehr der Fronttruppen;* volume III: *Karl und Rosa*. All quotes are from this edition.

18. For a sketch of the narrative, see Döblin's letter to Viktor Zukkerkandl dated February 3, 1939, Br, 231 f.

19. The fact that, at this time, Döblin dealt intensively with mysticism and Christian philosophy is revealed in a letter he wrote to Elvira and Arthur Rosin in which he states: "I myself, that's right, have taken a stronger interest (compared with two or three years ago) in Christian mysticism and philosophy, in connection with Kierkegaard. Perhaps you already noticed it in my volume *Bürger und Soldaten 1918* (the figures Becker, Tauler). It appears even more broadly in the unpublished second volume. It is nothing more than my (or really the general) ceaseless discussion about the 'ego' and 'nature' " (letter dated September 17, 1941, Br, 258).

20. "Epilog," Al, 394 f.

21. See "Revolutionstage im Elsass," *Die Neue Rundschau*, XXX (1919), 164–172.

22. "Epilog," Al, 395.

23. Concerning the question as to whether a Christian may become

a revolutionary, see Döblin's essay "Christentum und Revolution" (Al, 379–383) where the problem of action and sacrifice is raised once again.

24. Döblin himself stated that Becker goes a way "which for him personally is tragic and, objectively, leads into a cul-de-sac." (Letter to Irma Loos dated November 28, 1951, Br, 439).

Chapter Eight

1. Letter dated November 19, 1951, Br, 436.
2. Letter to Elvira and Arthur Rosin dated March 10, 1947, Br, 366.
3. I fully concur with the critical remarks which Döblin's friend Hermann Kasack made in a letter. The letter, dated February 29, 1947, is quoted Br, 616.
4. A similar melting process is also visible in the last dictations of Döblin, even though here his philosophy of nature seems to stand more in the foreground. See "Von Leben und Tod, die es beide nicht gibt," *Sinn und Form*, IX (1957), 902–933.
5. James Hilton's novel *Random Harvest*. See the letter to Elvira and Arthur Rosin dated July 11, 1941, Br, 253 f.
6. After almost fatal arguments with his wife, Erna, Döblin made a confession to his Parisian friend Robert Minder in May of 1955. In this context, Minder speaks about the "more than forty-year-old love-hate relationship to a spouse from whom he could not tear himself away." See Robert Minder, "Die Segelfahrt von Alfred Döblin. Struktur und Erlebnis. Mit unbekanntem biographischen Material," *Gestaltungsgeschichte und Gesellschaftsgeschichte* (Stuttgart, 1969), p. 477.
7. See the afterword by Heinz Graber "Zum Text der Ausgabe," *Hamlet*, p. 595.

Chapter Nine

1. On this point, see Manfred Durzak, "Flake und Döblin. Ein Kapitel aus der Geschichte des polyhistorischen Romans," *Germanisch-Romanische Monatsschrift*, XX (1970), 286–305.

Selected Bibliography

BIBLIOGRAPHIES

PEITZ, WOLFGANG. Alfred Döblin Bibliographie 1905–1970. Freiburg i. Br.: Becksmann, 1973. Tl. 1 Das Werk; Tl. 2 Sekundärliteratur. The most up-to-date, indispensable bibliography of Döblin's works and of secondary literature.

HAMELAU, KARIN. "Auswahlbibliographie zu Alfred Döblin," *Text und Kritik*, 13/14 (June 1966), 69–75. A very useful, carefully selected bibliography.

RILEY, ANTHONY W. In: *Jahrbuch der deutschen Schillergesellschaft*, XIV (1970), 637–661. A description of Döblin's literary remains in the Marbach Literatur-Archiv.

PRIMARY SOURCES

There is no complete edition of Döblin's works. The *Ausgewählte Werke in Einzelbänden* (in *Verbindung mit den Söhnen des Dichters*, edited by Walter Muschg; Olten/Freiburg i. Br.: Walter, 1960 ff.) have been appearing since 1960. Since Muschg's death in 1965, this edition has been continued by Heinz Graber. Up to now the following volumes, each containing an instructive postscript, have appeared:

1. *Pardon wird nicht gegeben*. 1960; 2nd ed. 1962.
2. *Die drei Sprünge des Wang-lun. Chinesischer Roman*. 1960.
3. *Berlin Alexanderplatz. Die Geschichte vom Franz Biberkopf*. 1961; 2nd ed. 1964. In the present volume the following translation is quoted: *Alexanderplatz, Berlin. The Story of Franz Biberkopf*, tr. Eugene Jolas. New York: The Viking Press, 1931; reprinted 1959.
4. *Manas. Epische Dichtung*. 1961.
5. *Babylonische Wandrung oder Hochmut kommt vor dem Fall*. 1962.
6. *Die Ermordung einer Butterblume. Ausgewählte Erzählungen 1910 bis 1950*. 1962.
7. *Amazonas*. 1963.
8. *Aufsätze zur Literatur*. 1963.
9. *Unser Dasein*. 1964.

10. *Wallenstein.* 1965.
11. *Hamlet oder die lange Nacht nimmt ein Ende.* 1966.
12. *Reise in Polen.* 1968.
13. *Briefe.* 1970.
14. *Schriften zur Politik und Gesellschaft.* 1972.
Additional volumes are in preparation. Besides the *Ausgewählte Werke* there also appeared: *Die Zeitlupe. Kleine Prosa,* posthumously edited by Walter Muschg. Olten/Freiburg i. Br.: Walter, 1962.
Doktor Döblin. Selbstbiographie, ed. Heinz Graber. Berlin: Friedenauer Presse, 1970.
Sämtliche Erzählungen. Reinbek bei Hamburg: Rowohlt, 1971.
The numerous special editions and paperbacks (above all, of *Berlin Alexanderplatz*) can not be listed here. For relevant information, see the bibliography of Wolfgang Peitz listed above.
My quotations are taken from the *Ausgewählte Werke* or—where that was impossible—from the following editions:
Wadzeks Kampf mit der Dampfturbine. Berlin: S. Fischer, 1918.
Der schwarze Vorhang. Roman von den Worten und Zufällen. Berlin: S. Fischer, 1919.
Der deutsche Maskenball. Zeitglossen (published under the pseudonym Linke Poot). Berlin: S. Fischer, 1921.
Berge Meere und Giganten. Berlin: S. Fischer, 1924.
Das Ich über der Natur. Berlin: S. Fischer, 1927.
Alfred Döblin. Im Buch. Zu Haus. Auf der Strasse, presented by Alfred Döblin and Oskar Loerke. Berlin: S. Fischer, 1928.
Wissen und Verändern! Offene Briefe an einen jungen Menschen. Berlin: S. Fischer, 1931.
Giganten. Abenteuerbuch. Berlin: S. Fischer, 1932.
Der Oberst und der Dichter oder das menschliche Herz. Freiburg i. Br.: K. Alber, 1946.
Unsere Sorge, der Mensch. Munich: K. Alber, 1948.
Der neue Urwald (Teil III der Südamerika Trilogie). Baden-Baden: Keppler, 1948.
Der unsterbliche Mensch. Ein Religionsgespräch (Herder Bücherei 41). Basel/Freiburg i. Br./Wien: Herder, 1948.
November 1918. Eine deutsche Revolution. Erzählwerk. Band I. Verratenes Volk. Munich: K. Alber, 1948.
November 1918. Band II. Heimkehr der Fronttruppen. Munich: K. Alber, 1949.
November 1918. Band III. Karl und Rosa. Munich: K. Alber, 1950.
Schicksalsreise. Bericht und Bekenntnis. Frankfurt/Main: Verlag Knecht-Carolusdruckerei, 1949.

Selected Bibliography

SECONDARY SOURCES

Books

KREUTZER, LEO. *Alfred Döblin. Sein Werk bis 1933* (Sprache und Literatur 66). Stuttgart: Kohlhammer, 1970. Interpretation of Döblin's work from its beginnings until the emigration, with particular emphasis on the politico-social aspect of his life and work.

RIBBAT, ERNST. *Die Wahrheit des Lebens im frühen Werk Alfred Döblins* (Münstersche Beiträge zur deutschen Literaturwissenschaft 4). Münster: Aschendorff, 1970. Extensive study of the early works, especially of the stories and early novels, above all in the context of the philosophy of nature and life.

WEYEMBERGH-BOUSSART, MONIQUE. *Alfred Döblin. Seine Religiosität in Persönlichkeit und Werk* (Abhandlungen zur Kunst-, Musik- und Literaturwissenschaft 76). Bonn: Bouvier, 1970. Comprehensive and extensive study of the complete *oeuvre* with special emphasis on religious and philosophical development.

Essays

ANDERS, GÜNTHER. "Der verwüstete Mensch. Über Welt- und Sprachlosigkeit in Döblins *Berlin Alexanderplatz*," *Festschrift für Georg Lukacs*, ed. F. Benseler. Neuwied/Berlin: Luchterhand, 1965. Pp. 420–442.

ARNOLD, ARMIN. "Der neue Mensch als Gigant: Döblins frühe Romane," *Die Literatur des Expressionismus. Sprachliche und thematische Quellen* (Sprache und Literatur 35), Armin Arnold, Stuttgart: Kohlhammer, 1966. Pp. 80–107.

BENJAMIN, WALTER. "Krisis des Romans. Zu Döblins *Alexanderplatz*," *Angelus Novus. Ausgewählte Schriften*, II, Walter Benjamin. Frankfurt/Main: Suhrkamp, 1966. Pp. 437–443.

CASEY, TIMOTHY JOSEPH. "Alfred Döblin," *Expressionismus als Literatur. Gesammelte Studien*, ed. Wolfgang Rothe. Bern/Munich: Francke, 1966. Pp. 637–655.

DURZAK, MANFRED. "Flake und Döblin. Ein Kapitel aus der Geschichte des polyhistorischen Romans," *Germanisch-Romanische Monatsschrift*, XX (1970), 286–305.

DUWE, WILHELM. "Alfred Döblin. *Berlin Alexanderplatz*," *Ausdrucksformen deutscher Dichtung vom Naturalismus bis zur Gegenwart. Eine Stilgeschichte der Moderne*, Wilhelm Duwe. Berlin: E. Schmidt, 1965. Pp. 102–113.

———. "Alfred Döblin. *Hamlet oder die lange Nacht nimmt ein Ende*." Ibid., pp. 113–120.

HÜLSE, ERICH. "Alfred Döblin. *Berlin Alexanderplatz*," *Möglichkeiten des modernen deutschen Romans. Analysen und Interpretations-*

grundlagen zu Romanen von Thomas Mann, Alfred Döblin . . ., ed. Rudolf Geissler. Frankfurt/Main: Diesterweg, 4th ed. 1970. Pp. 45–101.

LOERKE, OSKAR. "Das bisherige Werk Alfred Döblins," *Alfred Döblin. Im Buch. Zu Haus. Auf der Strasse*, presented by Alfred Döblin and Oskar Loerke. Berlin: S. Fischer, 1928. Pp. 116–175. Under the title "Alfred Döblins Werk (1928). Zu seinem 50. Geburtstag" also in: Loerke. *Gedichte und Prosa*, ed. Peter Suhrkamp, II. Frankfurt/Main: Suhrkamp, 1958. Pp. 560–604.

LÜTH, PAUL E. H. (ed.). *Alfred Döblin zum 70. Geburstag*. Wiesbaden: Limes, 1948.

MARTINI, FRITZ. "Alfred Döblin," *Deutsche Dichter der Moderne*, ed. Benno von Wiese. Berlin: E. Schmidt, 1965. Pp. 321–360.

———. "Alfred Döblin. Berlin Alexanderplatz," *Das Wagnis der Sprache. Interpretationen deutscher Prosa von Nietsche bis Benn*, Fritz Martini. Stuttgart: Klett, 2nd ed. 1956. Pp. 336–372.

MINDER, ROBERT. "Alfred Döblin," *Deutsche Literatur im XX. Jahrhundert*, ed. Otto Mann and Wolfgang Rothe, II, *Gestalten*. Bern/Munich: Francke, 5th ed. 1967. Pp. 126–150.

———. "Alfred Döblin zwischen Osten und Westen," *Dichter in der Gesellschaft*, Robert Minder. Frankfurt/Main: Insel, 1966. Pp. 155–190.

MUSCHG, WALTER. "Zwei Romane Alfred Döblins," *Von Trakl zu Brecht. Dichter des Expressionismus*, Walter Muschg. Munich: Piper, 1963. Pp. 198–243. Identical with the Afterwords to *Die drei Sprünge des Wang-lun* and *Berlin Alexanderplatz* in the *Ausgewählte Werke in Einzelbänden*.

———. "Ein Flüchtling. Alfred Döblins Bekehrung," *Die Zerstörung der deutschen Literatur* (List Bücher 156), Walter Muschg. Munich: List, no date. Pp. 87–111.

SCHÖNE, ALBRECHT. "Alfred Döblin. Berlin Alexanderplatz," *Der deutsche Roman*, ed. Benno von Wiese, II. Düsseldorf: Bagel, 1963. Pp. 291–325.

STRELKA, JOSEF. "Der Erzähler Alfred Döblin," *The German Quarterly*, XXXIII (1960), 197–210.

WALTER, HANS-ALBERT. "Alfred Döblin. Wege und Irrwege. Hinweise auf ein Werk und eine Edition," *Frankfurter Hefte*, XIX (1964), 866–878.

After the completion of this monograph, the following important studies of Döblin's work wre published:

MÜLLER-SALGET, KLAUS. Alfred Döblin. Werk und Entwicklung. Bonn: Bouvier, 1972.

PRANGEL, MATTHIAS. Alfred Döblin (Sammlung Metzler Band 105). Stuttgart: Metzler, 1973.

Index

Alfred Döblin Im Buch. Zu Haus. Auf der Strabe, 48, 155
Amazonas, 119–27, 135, 157
Anders, Günther, 161
Arnold, Armin, 43, 150, 161

Babylonische Wandrung, 111–16, 135, 136, 140
Bakunin, Mikhail, 25
Balzac, Honoré de, 115
Baudelaire, Charles, 115
Becher, Johannes R., 27, 32
Benjamin, Walter, 161
Benn, Gottfried, 32, 43, 61, 150
Berge Meere und Giganten, 26, 42, 64, 78–90, 92, 97, 115, 122, 124, 153, 154
Berlin Alexanderplatz, 27, 29, 44, 46, 66, 88, 99–109, 111, 112, 115, 129, 135, 137, 145, 148, 149, 156
Bernanos, George, 115
Binswanger, Ludwig, 29
Blewitt, Phyllis and Traver, 116
Brahms, Johannes, 34
Brecht, Bertolt, 26, 28, 31, 32, 47, 60, 104, 110
Broch, Hermann, 144
Bronnen, Arnolt, 26
Bruno, Giordano, 124, 125
Buber, Martin, 151, 152
Buddha, Gautama Siddhartha, 81, 91, 92, 154
Büchner, Georg, 77

Casey, Timothy J., 161
Christ, 93, 127, 128, 132
Confucius, 55, 151, 152

Corneille, Pierre, 116
Cortes, Hernando, 120

Das goldene Tor, 32
Das Ich über der Natur, 26, 48–53, 69, 81, 110, 125, 150
Dehmel, Richard, 20, 24
Denkler, Horst, 149
Der deutsche Maskenball, 25, 73, 79, 120
Der neue Urwald, 120, 124–27
Der Oberst und der Dichter, 136, 137
Der schwarze Vorhang, 36–39
Der Sturm, 34, 36, 41, 43, 47, 54, 93
Der unsterbliche Mensch, 128, 137
Die drei Sprünge des Wang-lun, 22 40, 54–65, 68, 69, 72, 90, 107, 112, 119
Die Ehe, 110
Die Ermordung einer Butterblume, 40
Die Linkskurve, 27
Die Literarische Welt, 26
Die Lobensteiner reisen nach Böhmen, 40
Die Nonnen von Kemnade, 78
Dostoevski, Feodor Mihailovich, 23, 34
Durzak, Manfred, 150, 158, 161
Duwe, Wilhelm, 161
Duytschaever, Joris, 155

Ebert, Friedrich, 130, 131
Ehrenstein, Albert, 150
Einstein, Albert, 48

Elshorst, Hansjörg, 152

Fechter, Paul, 115
Feuchtwanger, Lion, 31
Fischer, Samuel, 29
Flake, Otto, 144, 150
Flaubert, Gustave, 115
Flucht und Sammlung des Judenvolkes, 30
France, Anatole, 115
François-Poncet, André, 29
Freud, Sigmund, 34
Freudenheim, Sophie, 18, 21
Friedland, 30
Frisch, Efraim, 24, 148, 153

Galileo, 124
George, Stefan, 20
Giganten, 88–90
Giraudoux, Jean, 31
Glasenapp, Helmut von, 154
Goethe, Johann Wolfgang, 50, 55, 81, 135
Gollong, Heinz, 156
Graber, Heinz, 154, 155, 158, 159
Grass, Günter, 70, 153
Grothe, Wolfgang, 150

Halla, Ludwig, 154
Hamelau, Karin, 159
Hamlet oder die lange Nacht nimmt ein Ende, 18, 22, 116, 132, 136–43
Hauptmann, Gerhart, 20, 120
Hebbel, Freidrich, 102
Hegel, Georg Wilhelm Freidrich, 34
Hille, Peter, 20
Hilton, James, 158
Hitler, Adolf, 27, 131, 156
Hocke, Gustav René, 27
Hölderlin, Freidrich, 20, 34, 35
Hülse, Erich, 161
Huguet, Louis, 147

"Jagende Rosse," 19, 35, 36, 38
Jolas, Eugene, 159
Joyce, James, 105, 156
Jüdische Erneuerung, 30
Juncker, Axel, 149

Kafka, Franz, 54, 64
Kasack, Hermann, 158
Kepler, Johannes, 124
Kesten, Hermann, 147
Kierkegaard, Sören, 119, 139, 157
Kimber, Robert Bruce, 150, 151
Kirchner, Ernst Ludwig, 40
Kleist, Heinrich von, 20, 23, 34, 38, 104, 156
Kollwitz, Käthe, 29
Korsch, Karl, 28
Kreutzer, Leo, 20, 147, 148, 152, 153, 161
Kropotkin, Peter Alekseyevich, 25

Lao Tzu, 55, 61
Lasker-Schüler, Else, 20, 34, 35, 48
Lehmann, Wilhelm, 148
Lessing, Gotthold Ephraim, 46
Liebknecht, Karl, 131
Lieh Tzu, 54, 63
Links, Roland, 152
Lion, Ferdinand, 26, 155, 156
Lipschitz, Isidor, 30
Loerke, Oskar, 29, 54, 155, 162
Loos, Irma, 158
Ludwig, Otto, 156
Lusitania, 78
Lüth, Paul, 149, 155, 162
Luther, Martin, 23
Luxemburg, Rosa, 131
Lyck, Hugo, 116
Lydia und Mäxchen, 38, 39, 147

Manas, 26, 90–99
Mann, Heinrich, 29, 31
Mann, Thomas, 20, 31, 32, 144, 149
Marinetti, Filippo Tommaso, 43, 64, 65, 82
Martini, Fritz, 162
Mauthner, Fritz, 19, 52, 99, 149
Meyer, Albert Richard, 40
Michelangelo Buonarotti, 141
Minder, Robert, 31, 147, 154, 158, 162
Müller-Salget, Klaus, 162
Muschg, Walter, 124, 151, 157, 159, 162
Musil, Robert, 97, 144, 155

Index

Newton, Isaac, 104
Niclas, Yolla, 26, 86
Nietzsche, Freidrich, 34, 48, 145
November 1918, 25, 119, 127–35, 157

Osterle, Heinz Dieter, 156

Pardon wird nicht gegeben, 18, 110, 115–19
Pascal, Blaise, 116
Peitz, Wolfgang, 99, 155, 159
Petersen, Julius, 26, 155, 156
Pirandello, Luigi, 39
Piscator, Erwin, 110
Prangel, Matthias, 162
Proust, Marcel, 115

Ribbat, Ernst, 149, 150, 161
Reid, James H., 156
Reiss, Erna, 21, 22, 40, 118
Riley, Anthony W., 149, 159
Rilla, Paul, 149
Rolland, Romain, 115
Rosin, Arthur and Elvira, 147, 149, 156–58

Scheerbart, Paul, 19, 20, 38
Schicksalsreise, 17, 31, 111, 136, 147
Schlagintweit, Emil, 154
Schöne, Albrecht, 162
Schopenhauer, Arthur, 20, 74
Schuster, Ingrid, 151
Schwitters, Kurt, 103
Shakespeare, William, 138
Shiva, 90, 91, 94, 95, 98, 99
Spielhagen, Freidrich, 45

Spinoza, Baruch, 20
Stendhal, 115, 116
Stenzel, Jürgen, 155
Strelka, Josef, 162
Swinburne, Algernon Charles, 139

Tauler, Johannes, 129, 133, 134, 157
Toch, Ernst, 49
Tolstoy, Lev Nikolayevich, 23, 80

Unser Dasein, 48–53, 110, 115, 150

Verdi, Giuseppe, 26
Verne, Jules, 81

Wadzeks Kampf mit der Dampfturbine, 65–69, 112, 140, 152
Wagner, Richard, 34, 41
Walden, Herwarth, 20, 34, 35, 150, 153, 156
Wallenstein, 22, 60, 70–78, 156
Walter, Hans-Albert, 162
Wedekind, Frank, 20
Werfel, Franz, 26, 31
Weyembergh-Boussart, Monique, 151, 161
Wilhelm, Richard, 54
Wilson, Woodrow, 128
Wissen und Verändern!, 27, 30, 110
Wolf, Hugo, 34

Ziolkowski, Theodore, 100, 155, 156
Zmegač, Viktor, 150
Zuckerkandl, Viktor, 157
Zweig, Arnold, 136
Zwingli, Ulrich, 113